Half-title: *Sunrise over Annapurna South in central Nepal.*
Frontispiece: *The beauty and grace of a young Nepalese girl and her baby brother in Bhaktapur, Nepal.*
Page 4-5: *Kumari's consorts, Bhairab and Ganesh, survey the crowds from the windows of the Kumari's palace during Indra Jatra Festival in Kathmandu, Nepal.*
Page 6: *An elaborately carved wooden door of the Palace of the Fifty-Five Windows in Bhaktapur, Nepal.*
Page 8-9: *Tibetan families and monks of the Gelukpa sect walk around the stupa at Boudhanath as part of their New Year observances in the Kathmandu Valley, Nepal.*

PHOTO CREDITS

All photographs in this book are from **ANA Press Agency**: pages 32 (centre left), 43, 48 (top left), 54 (top left), 70 (centre) and 115 (centre); **Richard I'Anson**: pages 1, 11, 18, 26, 27 (centre right), 29 (top right), 34, 44 (top left), 46 (bottom left), 78-79, 81 (top left, centre right and bottom left), 89, 90 (middle left), 95 (bottom right), 103 (bottom), 107 (bottom), 108, 119, 121 (top left), 127 (bottom left) and back cover; **Bes Stock**: pages 29 (centre right), 49 (top left), 55 (centre), 68 (bottom left), 74, 77 (bottom left) and 82 (top left); **Jon Burbank**: pages 8-9, 25 (bottom), 28 (insets: top left and right), 29 (bottom centre), 36 (bottom left), 48 (bottom), 57 (bottom left and middle right), 61, 62 (2nd row, centre), 75 (centre), 77 (centre and bottom centre), 80, 88 (bottom left and top right), 92 (top left), 94 (bottom right), 109 (top left), 110 (centre and bottom right), 113 (top), 126 (top right) and 127 (centre left and bottom right); **Camera Press Ltd**: page 111 (top right and bottom); **the collection of Kiran Man Chitrakar, Ganesh Photo, Kathmandu**: pages 14 and 54 (bottom left and right); **Christine Osborne Pictures**: pages 36 (top right), 65 (bottom), 82 (bottom), 92 (top right), 113 (bottom right), 134, Nick Dawson — pages 36 (top left), 69, 73 (top left), 77 (top right), 86 (bottom left) and 93 (middle right and bottom right), Ann Cook — page 122 (top), C. Milne — pages 16-17; **HBL Network Photo Agency**: pages 6, 24 (bottom right and left), 25 (top), 27 (top right), 32 (top left), 33 (top), 38, 46 (bottom right), 47, 55 (top left), 62 (2nd row, right and 3rd row, left), 70 (top right and bottom right), 71 (centre), 73 (bottom right), 75 (bottom right), 84 (top left), 94 (middle left) 107 (centre right), 114 (bottom left), 130 and 138; **Dave G. Houser**: page 72 (centre left); **Hutchinson Library**: pages 44 (bottom left), 45 (bottom left and middle right), 46 (top left), 51 (middle right), 59 (top left), 68 (top left), 70 (bottom left), 75 (top left), 77 (top left), 92 (bottom), 101 (bottom centre), 118 (bottom left), 120, 133, 139 and 140; **John R. Jones**: pages 35 (top left), 40-41, 59 (top right), 62 (1st row, centre), 63 (centre), 104 (top left), 106, 111 (top left) and 144; **Earl Kowall**: pages 19, 24 (top left), 32 (bottom right), 37 (top right), 42 (bottom), 44 (top right), 45 (top left and right), 50 (top right), 51 (top left and right), 57 (bottom right), 59 (bottom), 62 (3rd row, centre), 65 (top right), 71 (top left), 82 (top right), 84 (bottom), 85 (top); 93 (bottom left), 95 (top right), 101 (top left), 105 (top), 111 (centre), 112 (top right), 113 (bottom centre), 114 (top right), 115 (bottom centre), 118 (centre right and bottom right), 121 (centre), 124 (bottom right), 126 (top left), 129 and 131; **Earl & Nazima Kowall**: pages 45 (middle left), 49 (bottom), 58, 65 (top right) and 76; **Nazima Kowall**: pages 10, 28 (main picture), 30-31, 33 (bottom right), 42 (top left), 45 (bottom right), 46 (top right), 49 (centre), 53 (centre), 54 (centre), 57 (centre left), 62 (2nd row, left and 3rd row, right), 63 (bottom right), 68 (middle left), 71 (top right), 72 (top right and main picture), 90 (middle right), 94 (bottom centre), 95 (top left), 115 (bottom right), 116 (bottom left and right), 121 (bottom right), 124 (bottom left), 125 (bottom right), 127 (centre right) and front and back end papers; **Jimmy Lam**: front cover, pages 27 (bottom left), 35 (bottom), 44 (bottom centre), 48 (top right), 63 (top left), 65 (centre), 73 (top right), 75 (top right), 83 (top right and bottom right), 85 (bottom right), 90 (bottom left), 97, 98, 101 (centre), 103 (top left), 104 (bottom), 105 (centre and middle right), 112 (bottom), 122 (bottom), 123 (centre), 124 (top), 125 (top right) and 126 (bottom); **Oldfield**: page 13; **Photobank Photolibrary Singapore**: pages 20-21, 59 (middle right), 71 (bottom centre), 85 (middle right), 99, 100, 102 and 118 (top left); **Morten Strange**: page 53 (top right); **Tan Chung Lee**: page 81 (top right); **Topham Picturepoint**: pages 12, 15 (bottom right), 46 (centre right), 52 (top left), 53 (top left), 56 (top left and centre), 57 (top left and right), 73 (middle right), 88 (top left), 114 (middle left and bottom right), 117 (top left) and 135; **Trip Photo Library**: pages 22 (main picture), 23 (inset: top right), 37 (bottom), 42 (centre left), 50 (bottom), 52 (bottom), 53 (bottom), 56 (bottom left), 64, 66-67, 90 (bottom right), 95 (middle right), 96 (top right), 109 (bottom), 114 (top left), 141, 142 and 143; **Vision Photo Agency/Hulton Getty**: pages 15 (top left) and 22 (inset: bottom right and left); **Nik Wheeler**: pages 52 (top right), 62 (1st row, left and right), 71 (bottom left), 90 (top left and right), 91, 94 (top left), 95 (bottom left) and 125 (centre); **Alison Wright**: pages 2, 4-5, 35 (top right), 39, 49 (top right), 50 (top left), 51 (bottom right), 55 (bottom), 60, 63 (bottom left), 68 (bottom right), 75 (bottom), 86 (centre left), 87, 88 (middle left and bottom right), 93 (top), 94 (top right), 101 (top right and bottom right), 103 (top right), 104 (top right), 105 (bottom right), 107 (top left and middle left), 109 (centre), 110 (top left and bottom centre), 112 (top left and middle left), 113 (centre right and centre left), 115 (top left), 116 (top right), 117 (top right and bottom left), 121 (bottom centre), 123 (bottom centre), 125 (bottom left), 127 (top left), 132, 136 and 137.

HIMALAYAN KINGDOM: ROOF OF THE WORLD

© 2000 Times Media Private Limited

Published by Times Editions
An imprint of Times Media Private Limited
A member of the Times Publishing Group
Times Centre, 1 New Industrial Road
Singapore 536196

Designer: Tuck Loong
Editor: Paul Rozario
Picture Researcher: Susan Jane A. Manuel
Production Manager: Anthoney Chua
Colour separation by United Graphic Pte Ltd, Singapore
Printed in Singapore

All rights reserved. No part of this publication may be reproduced, stored in a retrieval system or transmitted, in any form or by any means, electronic, mechanical, photocopying, recording or otherwise, without the persmission of the copyright owner.

ISBN: 981 232 140 3

HIMALAYAN KINGDOM
ROOF OF THE WORLD

HIMALAYAN KINGDOM
ROOF OF THE WORLD

Text
JON BURBANK

Times Editions

CONTENTS

INTRODUCTION 11
HISTORY AND THE HIMALAYAS 13

PART ONE
A COLLISION OF CONTINENTS 19
Mountain Grandeur 20
A Question of Altitude 27
Rivers and Rain 35

PART TWO
FLORA AND FAUNA 39
Riches and Rarities 40
Spiritual Anchors 49
Birds of the Heights 53
The Inevitable Conflict 54
Of Reality and Myth 56

PART THREE
PEOPLE, CUSTOMS AND BELIEFS 61
Tolerant World 63
A Test of Faith 65
Ancient Beliefs 75
Marking the Way 84
Food and Life 90
A Noble Obsession 96

PART FOUR
ANONYMITY AND DEVOTION 99
Protection and Piety 101
Newar Architecture 109
Sculpture 112
Originality Within Convention 116
Whirls of Colour and Passion 123
A Living Tradition 127

Map 128
Sacred Art of the Middle Way 129

INTRODUCTION

A rock wall 8,000 metres high fills your vision. In the pre-dawn light its ice and snow mantle is all muted shades of blue and grey. Suddenly, a single point of gold bursts on the horizon. It sweeps down the slopes, changing from a blinding brilliance to a golden luminescence. Freud speaks of places of pilgrimage, landscapes where we relinquish our discrete identities and envelop ourselves in an 'oceanic feeling' which for him was the equivalent of religious belief. Watching that dawn caress the face of Mount Annapurna in Nepal, you experience just such an 'oceanic feeling', for all around you lies the Himalayan Kingdom, the highest point on the planet, the Roof of the World.

Sacred sites abound in this mountainous terrain. In western Tibet sits Mount Kailash, considered 'the navel of the world'. It is a treasured place of pilgrimage for both Hindus and Buddhists. Thirty kilometres due north beyond Annapurna's golden wall lies Muktinath. It is known as the 'place of salvation', for the great 4th century B.C. Hindu epic, *Mahabharata*, teaches that to bathe in Muktinath's springs is to gain deliverance after death. It is here that Brahma, Hindu Creator of the Universe, lit a blue flame upon the waters as an offering. The flame still burns, protected within a Buddhist temple.

The Buddha was born by a pond in Lumbini, southern Nepal, under the gaze of the Himalayas. The religion that sprang from his words, however, spread beyond the snowy peaks to the Tibetan Plateau. Untouched by the monsoon winds which cannot breach the lofty Himalayas, the Tibetan Plateau is one of the harshest environments on earth, with little air, heat and rain. Yet somehow, in this land of numbing hardship there is a spiritual richness not often found elsewhere on earth.

Great *lamas*, or teachers of Buddhist doctrine, spread the religion to a small remote southeastern corner of the Himalayas where Tibetans had settled. A unique form of Buddhism appeared here in what is today's Bhutan: Drukpa Kagyu, or 'Whispered Transmission of the Dragon People'. This is a land of steep crags and valleys, of rich forests perched between soaring mountains and impenetrable jungle.

In Nepal people settled on the great swathe of steep hills that break against the Himalayas. The Aryan people from the south brought with them Hindu gods and a caste system. Having come from the wet Indian plains, they preferred the low river valleys that drained the Himalayan foothills. Mongoloid tribes from the north crossed the Himalayas and populated the highlands, bringing with them their Buddhist and highland culture. The two groups and their cultures survive intact to this day, with the result that crossing each ridge reveals a new culture and language. Kathmandu, Nepal's capital city, is a kaleidoscope of cultures and faiths and remains, despite the rush to modernise, a magical place.

Tibet, Nepal and Bhutan, with the lesser-known Indian regions of Ladakh and Sikkim — together they share the Himalayas, the greatest mountains on earth. Their cultures overlap but remain distinct. There exudes everywhere in the Himalayas the same spirit of tolerance. In a landscape that is both stunningly beautiful and frightfully arduous, people have managed to create rich cultures and heritages which they guard with an admirable pride and reverence.

An old monk of the Kagyupa sect (facing page) waits with bright yellow marigolds for the start of the cremation ceremonies of His Holiness the 16th Karmapa in Rumtek, Sikkim. West of Sikkim's Himalayas lies the Annapurna Range in Nepal. Its mountains, like Annapurna South and Hiunchuli (above), here seen from the town of Dhampus in Nepal, lie protected within the Annapurna Sanctuary.

HISTORY AND THE HIMALAYAS

It is A.D. 625. A young Nepalese princess pauses on a Himalayan pass. Her head pounds, her heart races. She breathes, but the air does not seem to come. She is lovely, her skin fair, her eyes large, accentuated by the kohl that lines them. Beneath her warm cloak flash gold and rich silks. Her earlobes hang low and sway with gold. Her name is Bhrikuti and she is not here by choice.

Her father, King Amsuvarman, has commanded her to take this difficult journey across the Himalayas to the Roof of the World. There she is to marry the Tibetan king, Songsten Gampo, the most feared man in Asia. King Amsuvarman can think of no other way to save his kingdom. Songsten's armies threaten not only Nepal, but also T'ang China. The T'ang emperor too has sent his daughter, Princess Wencheng, to marry and pacify the Tibetan monarch.

Both brides came with rich dowries. In hers Wencheng included a portrait of the Buddha. Bhrikuti is said to have had with her the Buddha's own begging bowl. Both princesses brought with them a faith in the Buddha's teachings so strong that they converted their warlike husband to the Middle Way. The two wives are remembered today as *bodhisattvas*, or enlightened beings. They are the two *Tara*, or Saviours, Bhrikuti the Green Tara and Wencheng the White.

Almost a millennium before Bhrikuti's journey, Ram came to the kingdom of Janakpur in Nepal's Terai lowlands. There he found his bride, the lovely and dutiful Sita. Their adventures, together with those of Ram's brother Lakshman and a faithful friend Hanuman, the Monkey King, took them to the isle of Lanka and back. Their story is immortalised in the ancient Hindu epic, the *Ramayana*.

Another hero of the Himalayas is Guru Rinpoche, credited with spreading Buddhism to the cold, windswept plains beyond the mountains. Born a prince in the early 8th century in the valley of the Swat River in Pakistan, he was educated by the wisest pundits in India. His life is now the stuff of legend.

One of Guru Rinpoche's many astounding miracles involved his father-in-law, the king of Zahor, who opposed the lama's union with his daughter, the beautiful Princess Mandarava. The angry king ordered them to be thrown alive into flames. Guru Rinpoche, uttering calm words, promptly turned the flaming pyre into a lake and converted the entire kingdom to Buddhism. Another time, Guru Rinpoche's own father, ashamed that his son had renounced the kingdom, ordered him to be burned alive. Once again Guru Rinpoche snuffed out the flames and reappeared sitting on a lotus in a lake. In this way did he win the title *Padmasambhava*, or 'Born of the Lotus'.

Yet another feat took place when Tibet's king asked for his help against the fierce demons, who each night would destroy the day's construction work on Samye Monastery. Typically, Guru Rinpoche did not vanquish the demons but converted them to Buddhism through his preaching and with the help of a handy *dorji*, a thunderbolt. The lama's words conquered entire kingdoms, defeated in debate hundreds of heretics who contested his teachings. He founded the Nyingmapa (red hat) sect that is still the sect followed by the Bhutanese monarchy. His preaching converted many all across the Himalayas.

Ram and Sita fly on Garuda's wings (facing page) in the Ramayana, or Romance of Ram. This Hindu epic is a source for Nepal's mythical past. Recent history is depicted in this print (above) by Oldfield, of Kathmandu's Durbar Square in the 1850s. The artist was one of the few Europeans allowed into Nepal at that time.

Tsongkhapa (1357–1419) came from a more humble background in eastern Tibet. He studied the various strains of contemporary Buddhist thought and synthesised them into what is now the Gelukpa (yellow hat) sect. His nephew, Genden Drup, founded a monastery and, more historically significant, announced that upon his death he would be reincarnated. His reincarnation, Genden Gyatso, enlarged the size and prestige of Gelukpa.

Genden Drup's third reincarnation, Sonam Gyatso, met with the Mongol Khan in 1578, and so impressed him that he was given the title *Ta-Le*, or 'Ocean of Wisdom'. Today Genden Drup's 13th reincarnation is the Dalai Lama, who in 1959 left Tibet following its occupation by Chinese troops. In 1989 he was awarded the Nobel Peace Prize for his efforts to solve Tibet's troubled situation.

Bhutan developed its counterpart to the Dalai Lama in the great Ngawang Namgyal (1594–1651). Scholar, painter, dancer, teacher, nation-builder and diplomat — Ngawang Namgyal was all this and more to Bhutan. His powerful oratory brought him religious and secular authority, from neither of which he shied away. He became the Shabdrung Rinpoche, the 'Precious Jewel at Whose Feet one Prostrates', and established Drukpa Kagyu as Bhutan's *de facto* state form of Buddhism.

Ngawang Namgyal unified the country and beat back a Tibetan invasion. In 1651, at the height of his power, he withdrew from public life to live as a hermit monk. He probably died shortly thereafter, but his death was not announced until 1705. This triggered off a period of instability that lasted until Ugyen Wangchuk consolidated power in the 1880s and formally became the Druk Gyalpo, or Dragon King, in 1907. His great-grandson Jigme Singye Wangchuk wears Bhutan's Raven Crown today.

Nepal's history too has its fair share of notable characters. When Prithvi Narayan Shah stood on the rim of the Kathmandu Valley in 1760 he saw a valley that glittered with golden-roofed temples and emerald green rice fields. The small valley held four tiny kingdoms ruled since the 15th century by relatives of a single family, the Mallas. They had prospered, but constant squabbling between brothers and cousins on thrones almost within sight of each other kept the valley fractured and disunited.

By this time, Prithvi Narayan Shah's own Rajput family had already been established in Nepal. Several centuries earlier they had been pushed out of Indian Rajasthan by Muslim conquerors. Shah decided that he would be the one to unite the valley. He embarked on a military campaign which eventually brought the Kathmandu Valley under his control in 1769. He was cruel in victory. Having conquered Kirtipur, he ordered the lips and noses of each man in the town to be cut off and tossed into a huge hideous pile. It is from this incident that Kirtipur earned its name as the City of Noses.

Jung Bahadur Rana (top right), the first of the Rana prime ministers of Nepal, visited Britain in the mid-19th century. He used the opportunity to learn about western norms. On his return to Nepal, he instituted a liberal revision of the criminal code, inaugurated the wearing of European dress at court and began building European-style palatial dwellings with imported material. He built dozens of grand Rana palaces. The reign of the Ranas came to an end a century later in 1951, when King Tribhuvan, pictured here as a boy (top left), deposed them with the help of Nepalese groups in India.

The Shah dynasty enlarged Nepal until its border stretched from Sikkim to Kashmir, an expansion curtailed by unsuccessful wars with Tibet and China. As a result, Nepal paid tribute to China until 1912. Nepal fared little better against the empire building British, losing to them in the early 19th century most of its valuable agricultural Terai lowlands. The British were so impressed with the fighting qualities of the Nepalese soldiers that they recruited them as the famous Gurkha mercenaries.

Embittered by defeat, the Nepalese closed off their country to European contact but for a British Resident. He watched the Nepalese court slide into power-grabbing intrigues culminating in the infamous Kot Massacre of September 14, 1846.

That night, a single shot killed the queen's lover in his chambers. As a monsoon storm howled and lightning crackled, the enraged queen gathered hundreds of court nobles into her chambers and demanded to know the identity of the murderer. Among them was a young schemer of ice-cold blood and great presence of mind: Jung Bahadur Rana. He discreetly brought his armed men inside and had them close the doors. What provoked the ensuing bloodbath is not known, but once it began Rana ordered his troops to kill everyone.

Following the elimination of most of the nobility, Rana and his successors ruled as *maharajahs*, or prime ministers, with the king a powerless figurehead. They treated the national treasury as their private bank account, continued Nepal's isolation from the rest of the world and had cars and Italian marble carried into the valley for their use. In 1950 the Nepalese king, Tribhuvan, loaded his family into a car and, on the pretext of going for a picnic, sped off into the compound of the Indian Embassy, to ask help to end the corrupt reign of the Ranas. The following year the Ranas fell from power, and Nepal is today a constitutional monarchy

European visitors started arriving as far back as Marco Polo, and a few deserve special note. In the early 1900s Sven Hedin, a Swede, personally mapped over 65,000 square miles of Tibet. He combined athletic endurance and limitless curiosity with extraordinary courage and a colossal ego. One of his greatest moments came in 1907 when, guided by three Tibetans, he entered the Kubi-Tsangpo Valley and found a 'world of gigantic peaks, black but covered with perpetual snow, pointed like wolves' teeth, mighty glacier tongues lying between them'.

That same year Hedin 'had the joy of being the first white man to penetrate to the source of the Brahmaputra and the Indus, the two rivers, famous since time immemorial, which like a crab's claw encircle the Himalayas'. He was also the first European to perform the circumambulatory pilgrimage round sacred Mount Kailash, Centre of the Universe.

What Hedin did for Himalayan geography, the Frenchwoman Alexandra David-Néel did for Himalayan anthropology. With fierce determination and a sparkling intellect, she turned herself into a Tibetan, studying language and culture, even spending months in a cave to study Buddhism. She made several attempts to enter Tibet, but was caught each time.

Finally, in the winter of 1923, accompanied by Yongden, a monk whom she later adopted as her son, she walked to Lhasa. Dyeing her hair with Chinese black ink and rubbing her face with soot from their cooking pot, she succeeded in passing herself off as the Tibetan mother of Yongden. She was also the first western woman to interview the Dalai Lama, while he was in exile in Darjeeling. She gives some of the best descriptions of the country she walked through:

'For miles we proceeded under cover of gloomy, silent and mysterious forests. Then, an unexpected clearing suddenly revealed, behind the dark line of tall fir trees, extraordinary landscapes of shining snow-clad mountains towering high in the blue sky, frozen torrents and glittering waterfalls hanging like gigantic and immaculate curtains from the rugged rocks. We looked at them, speechless and enraptured, wondering if we had not reached the confines of the human world and were confronted with the abode of some genie. Tomorrow or the day after a new fantastic apparition would rise before us in the same instantaneous way!'

The descriptions of the Himalayas by Sven Hedin (top left) and Alexandra David-Neél (right) are relatively recent ones. The Himalayas are extolled in ancient Indian writings such as the Vedas and the Puranas: 'A hundred divine epics would not suffice to describe all the marvels of the Himalayas...' (following pages); Kalidasa, the 5th century Indian poet, incorporates them into his love poetry: 'The Himalayan winds that plunder many a flower and hasten nectar-sweet towards the south cool my hot breast, delighting with the thought that once, perhaps not long ago, they touched thy limbs.'

PART ONE
A COLLISION OF CONTINENTS

Water from taps in Jomosom, northern Nepal, often flies out horizontally, disappearing in the wind before even reaching the ground. So strong and fierce is the wind, symbolised in Tibetan mythology by Longda, the Wind Horse. He races down from Tibet through the valley of the Kali-Gandaki River and into the deepest river gorge in the world. Walking the valley is a continuous struggle with the wind. Most of the time your eyes are watching your feet pick their way along the trail. Suddenly your eyes fall on a jet black rock. It is spherical and the size of an orange. You find a crack and the two halves open to reveal the perfect spiral of a fossilised ammonite shell. Three thousand metres above sea level, amidst the highest mountains in the world, you are holding the remains of a prehistoric creature whose natural habitat was the ocean seabed. You almost forget the wind.

Over 60 million years ago this area was indeed an ocean, part of the vast Tethys Sea (today's Mediterranean Sea is a remnant). The break-up of Gondwanaland marked the beginning of the end of the Tethys. Part of the proto-continent, what is now India, then began its slow course toward the Eurasian continent. Some 10 to 15 million years ago India and Asia finally collided. The Eurasian plate pushed the Indian plate down and under Asia. As the Indian plate went under, it forced the Asian plate upwards, buckling it. The process was marked by periodic bursts of intense uplift. The main upward thrust occurred just 600,000 years ago, making the Himalayas the youngest mountains in the world.

Standing in the howling wind, with 60 million years of history in your hand, you look over to the Kali-Gandaki River nearby. Further south, the river plunges between the Annapurna and Dhaulagiri mountains, both rising to a height of over 8,000 metres above sea level. The Kali-Gandaki is one of the few rivers that has been able to force its way right through the Himalayas. Most other rivers had to look for a way around them. The Brahmaputra had to run due east the entire length of Tibet and the northern edge of the Himalayas before cutting south into northeast India. Starting in almost the same place, the Ganges, holy river of Hinduism, first runs west in the opposite direction, then south through the mountains, and finally east along the southern edge of the Himalayas until it blends with the Brahmaputra in a great delta before flowing into the Bay of Bengal. Over millions of years the Ganges has wandered all over its vast plain, leaving behind the rich soil that makes the Terai lowlands so vital to Nepal and Bhutan. North of the Terai lowlands are the Middle Hills that lead to the Himalayas.

Looking north from the Kali-Gandaki, with the Annapurna Range behind, you are beyond the Himalayas, on the edge of the great Tibetan Plateau. This is the Roof of the World, a vast flat plain with an average elevation of over 4,000 metres above sea level. It is one of the harshest environments in the world, but standing in a wind that wants to push you over and seemingly tear skin from flesh, a wind so devoid of oxygen that breathing makes your lungs ache, that is something you already knew.

Trekkers (facing page) in central Nepal survey the splendour of the Annapurna Sanctuary, home to some of Nepal's highest mountains and a popular destination for tourists. Ladakh, in the northwestern Himalayas, has a landscape (above) that is dry and inhospitable and strongly resembles the surface of the moon.

MOUNTAIN GRANDEUR

The term 'plate tectonics' is used to describe the formation of the Himalayas. The word 'tectonics' originates from the ancient Greek word *tekton*, meaning 'builder'. This is a fitting description of the result of the collision of the Indian subcontinent with the Eurasian landmass. This collision caused the edge of the Eurasian plate to compress, buckle and 'build up' into the Himalayas. Himalaya originates from the Sanskrit *hima*, meaning 'snow', and *la*ya, 'dwelling place' or 'abode'. The Abode of Snows is an apt name for this range of snowy mountains that stretches for more than 2,400 kilometres. The Himalayas contain more than 30 peaks that rise to over 7,600 metres above sea level.

About one-third of the Himalayas lies within Nepal, which is without question at the heart of the range. Eight of the ten highest mountains in the world are in Nepal, including Mount Everest, which it shares with Tibet. At 8,852 metres above sea level, the summit of Everest is the highest point on earth. The second and third highest mountains in the world are also found in the Himalayas — Mount Godwin Austen(8,611 metres) in the Karakorams northwest of Ladakh, and Kanchenjunga(8,598 metres) in Sikkim, India.

The further east one travels in the Himalayas, the denser and more compact the mountains become, until, in Bhutan, they are a seemingly impenetrable jumble of high peaks and steep valleys. Bhutan is almost totally mountainous, with a fifth of the country under perpetual snow. It shares its highest mountain, 7,554-metre Kulha Gangri, with Tibet.

The Earth Mother

Early written accounts of attempts to scale Mount Everest are often written in a grand, panoramic style befitting the splendour of their subject. Of the tallest mountain in the world, one account states: 'there is no complication for the eye. The highest of the world's mountains has to make but a single gesture of magnificence to be lord of all, vast in unchallenged and isolated supremacy.' Yet Sir Francis Younghusband, the great English explorer, described Everest as 'a shy and retiring mountain'.

To the Himalayan people she is much more than a mountain; she is Chomolungma, or Sagarmatha, respectively the Tibetan and Sanskrit terms for 'Goddess-Mother-of-the-World'. For mere mortals to even approach her is considered sacrilegious. But today's 21st century climbers may say that Mount Everest does not dominate as one would expect, being surrounded by other visible giants.

Whatever the many moods or roles of this famous mountain, Everest exerts a powerful hold on the collective consciousness of mankind. Humbled and speechless before her, George Mallory, one of earliest Europeans to have a close-up view of the mountain in 1921, sums it up: 'We paused in sheer astonishment. The sight of it banished every thought; we asked no questions and made no comment, but simply looked …'

The majesty of the world's tallest mountain, Mount Everest (right), seen here from the Nepalese side. Held in reverence by Buddhists, Hindus and Tibetan Bon animists is Mount Kailash (facing page, top right), to which devotees of all three religions make pilgrimages.

The ones who made it and the ones who didn't. The photograph (far left) of Edmund Hillary and Tenzing Norgay was taken on their descent from Everest after they conquered the summit on 29th May 1953. Thirty years earlier George Mallory began his journey to the summit. He disappeared high on Everest. This photograph (left) is one of the last of him alive. He is standing second from the left. Mallory's body was found near the summit in 1999, 75 years after his disappearance. Researchers believe he fell whilst descending. Nobody knows if he reached the summit.

Centre of the Universe

Centre of the Universe, Navel of the World, Abode of the Gods — just some of the epithets given to Mount Kailash in western Tibet. Its hulking shape, four sheer faces aligning to the cardinal points and a dazzling snow-covered peak have all earned it the name Kang Rinpoche, Tibetan for 'Precious Jewel of Snow'.

Hindus link it to Mount Meru, the mythical peak that bridges heaven and earth, described in the *Mahabharata* as 'shining like the morning sun and, like a fire without smoke, immeasurable and unapproachable by men of manifold sins'.

Buddhists believe that Samvara, the wrathful form of Buddha, resides here. Hindus say Shiva, the destroyer and creator, lives on Kailash's snowy peak. Jains revere the mountain because their first saint received his earthly release on it. The animistic Bon worshippers of Tibet believe their founder Shenrab first alighted on Kailash when he descended from heaven.

The 53-kilometre circumambulation of Mount Kailash is the holiest pilgrimage a Tibetan Buddhist can make. Thousands undertake the pilgrimage during the full moon festival of Saga Dawa in May and June. Some pilgrims make the entire circuit by first prostrating themselves, then standing and placing their feet where their hands were, and then repeating the whole process. Hindus vie for the limited number of places given each year for them to make a similar pilgrimage to Kailash.

Five Treasuries of the Great Snow

Kanchenjunga, at 8,598 metres above sea level, is the world's third tallest mountain. It dominates Sikkim's Himalayas, towering 40 kilometres from Sikkim's capital, Gangtok. Most of Sikkim's population is settled in and around this town; little wonder then that the Sikkimese treat this awesome neighbour with reverence and respect as they go about their daily lives under its dominating hulk.

Kanchenjunga's name is derived from Tibetan and interpreted in Sikkim as the 'Five Treasuries of the Great Snow'. These five treasuries refer to the five peaks that compose Kanchenjunga's summit. Each peak represents a different treasure: salt, precious stone, religion, medicine and invincible armour. United in Kanchenjunga's five peaks, they depict important aspects of the Sikkimese worldview.

This sacred peak also represents both the god Kanchenjunga and his abode. Each New Year Kanchenjunga is worshipped during the Phanglhapsol Festival. The god is portrayed as a fiery, red-faced deity with a crown of five human skulls, riding the mythical snow lion and holding aloft the banner of victory. The monsoon rains he brings are both blessing and curse; they ensure not only a bountiful harvest but also death and destruction through floods and landslides. The mountain's ominous aura is enhanced by the legends of the *neeguyed* who inhabits its snowy slopes. This mysterious abominable snowman is more popularly known by his Sherpa title, *yeti*.

Straddling the border of Nepal and Sikkim, Mount Kanchenjunga (above) cuts a dramatic figure totally in keeping with its status as the world's third highest mountain. This particular view of the sacred summit is taken from Sandakpur in the state of West Bengal, which borders Sikkim in the south, and shows Janu Mountain on the left of the five peaks of the Kanchenjunga range.

Pilgrimage and Landscape

At Mount Kailash a figure wears a chest-to-ankles leather apron. On his hands are round leather pads. The pilgrim raises his padded hands over his head in prayer, then prostrates full length in the dirt, padded hands remaining outstretched. He rises, covered in dust, and then places his feet in the prints left by the pads. He prostrates on the ground again, repeating the process over and again until he has travelled the 53-kilometre *kora*, or pilgrimage route, around the mountain.

At nearby Lake Manasarowar, generally regarded as the highest freshwater lake in the world, Hindu pilgrims finally finish their days of walking and plunge into the icy waters for the bath that can wash away 100 lives' worth of sins. Both Hindus and Buddhists believe that to undertake hardship in the course of worship is to accumulate good *karma*, or merit, aiding the soul's slow climb to gain release from the cycle of life, death and rebirth.

*P*ilgrimage in the Himalayas: A pilgrim prays in the courtyard of Tashilunpho Monastery (above), 100 kilometres west of Lhasa, Tibet. Founded in 1447 it is the home monastery of the Panchen (Great Scholar) Lama, second in authority only to the Dalai Lama. The pilgrim's mat will protect him when he prostrates on the ground. The more austere practice of prostrating in the dirt without a mat is undertaken by this pilgrim (facing page, bottom right) beside the Yarlung Tsangpo river. He performs his devotions by a wall of mani stones carved and left by the generations of pilgrims who have passed this spot before him. Simple meals accompany pilgrims paths and food is cooked in the open (facing page, bottom left) en route to holy Mount Kailash. This sacred peak rises out of a dry barren landscape in the far southwest of Tibet, a landscape harsh even for Tibetans accustomed to arduous daily lives. Janakpur (left), a Nepalese town that lies southeast of Kathmandu in the Terai region, holds a special place in the hearts of the country's Hindus. This ancient city was named after King Janak, the father of the goddess Sita, who was the wife of Ram and heroine of the Ramayana. The ancient glory of Janakpur is preserved in its many sculpted ponds and baths, temples and palace ruins. The Sita Kund shown here is said to be the bathing pond of Sita and many pilgrims come to take holy baths in it.

A QUESTION OF ALTITUDE

Within the Himalayan Kingdom, particularly in Bhutan and Nepal, there is probably a greater variety of climate and ecology than over any other area of comparable size on earth. Tropical, temperate, alpine and arctic environments are all well represented.

It is all a question of altitude, which in Nepal varies quickly and dramatically. A trekker can move from a subtropical to an alpine habitat within a single day, first passing rice fields, banana trees and tigers, and, within a few hours, reaching pine forests, barley fields and rock-strewn ridges that are home to the elusive snow leopard.

Elevations in Bhutan and Nepal vary from 100 metres above sea level to nearly 9,000 metres at Mount Everest. Mountains and hills leap up, plunge down and then leap up again.

In Ladakh, where we find some of the highest mountain passes in the world, cultivated green fields lie in valley floors above which loom steep, barren slopes. Visitors there are struck by the stark juxtaposition of fertility and wasteland.

Sikkim has little lowland and its variation in relief is extreme, rising from an elevation of 230 metres in the Tista River valley to 8,598 metres above sea level at Kanchenjunga, all within the short distance of 80 kilometres.

The question of altitude distinguishes not just natural habitats, but people and traditions as well. Hindus tend to live at lower elevations, closer to their Indian origins in the south. Buddhists, on the other hand, prefer higher elevations, nearer their Tibetan counterparts.

Altitudes fluctuate with each peak and valley in the Himalayas. This causes a great deal of discomfort to travellers unused to frequent changes in air pressure. However, these rapidly fluctuating heights support an amazingly rich ecosystem and provide some breathtaking panoramas. The hillside forests of Gunsa (facing page) on the Nepalese side of Kanchenjunga come alive in beautiful autumnal colours, while the slopes at higher altitudes in the background are barren and brown. A similar variety of landscapes presents itself below snow-covered Kangbochen peak (top right) in Peiku Tso, Tibet, where a large expanse of desert separates fertile riverbanks from the mountain. The central Nepalese Gurung village of Ghandruk (above) sits in the shadow of snowy Annapurna, which is named after the Goddess of Grain. The lush greenery around the homesteads contrasts with the cold dry slopes that are just a stone's throw away on the other side of Annapurna. A rocky stream (left) winds its way through lush forests in Bhutan, while the sun reflects brightly off the snowy eastern Himalayas looming high above in the background.

The Terai Lowlands

The Terai is the low flat plain of the Ganges River as it washes onto the rugged hills that mark the beginning of the massive collision of the Indian and Asian plates. At elevations above sea level of 100 metres or less, it is the only flat area of Nepal and characterised by an almost imperceptible gradient.

In Bhutan the Terai blends into the Duars, Sanskrit for 'gate', which are low river valleys leading into the hills. These lowland areas make up only a small portion of the Himalayas, but have an importance that far outstrips their modest size. The warm climate and fertile alluvial soil, well-watered by the monsoon, make the Terai lowlands ideal for rice cultivation.

For much of history the lowlands were a thick jungle that represented an impenetrable barrier to outsiders. Fear of elephants, tigers and cobras kept people out. The Terai's most effective deterrent was a particularly virulent strain of malaria carried by thick clouds of mosquitoes. In Nepal the jungle was inhabited by the Tharu tribe who had somehow developed an immunity to this form of malaria.

In the 1950s large parts of the jungle were cleared and settled, with DDT eradicating most of the mosquitoes. Today about half of Nepal's population lives here and it is by far the most economically dynamic part of the country.

Sikkim has another name — Denzong — which means 'Valley of Rice'. The monsoon-flooded rice terraces (right) in the Saramsa Valley bear testimony to the bounty of Sikkim's few lowland areas. Nepal has more significant lowlands called the Terai. These flat expanses along the southern border with India, such as at Narayanghat in the Chitwan region (top, left and right inset), are covered with green rice fields come monsoon time.

The Middle Hills

The Himalayas do not spring up directly from the plain of the Ganges River. In between the white peaks and the fertile plain of the Terai lowlands are row after row of high ridges that range in height from about 1,000 to 3,000 metres above sea level. These are the Middle Hills. In both Bhutan and Nepal they are the single largest topographical feature, constituting about half the land mass.

Geography influences culture here; the Middle Hills mark clearly the ethnic divisions in Nepal. Hindus of Indian origin, whose ancestors had come from the south centuries ago, have remained at the foothills, close to the lowlands reminiscent of their ancestral homes. The descendants of the hill tribes, whose forefathers had crossed the Himalayas from the north, again generations ago, continue to inhabit the higher ridges where their ancestors had settled.

The Middle Hills are the cultural heartland of the Himalayas, moulding the character of its people. The capitals of Bhutan and Nepal, Thimphu and Kathmandu respectively, both lie in valleys of the Middle Hills. While the mountains are remote, a source of reflection and meditation, the Middle Hills represent familiarity, home and food security.

Winter sees the hills fade to a dull brown from lack of rain. But they glow a vibrant green later with the summer monsoon. Terraced rice fields built up over many years cascade down for hundreds of metres. Each morning people make the long walk down to their terraces, each evening they climb back up again.

The land near Bhaktapur (above) in the Kathmandu Valley, Nepal, has been farmed for hundreds if not thousands of years. It has been broken up again and again while being handed down from fathers to sons. Worked by men and not machines, the land evolves continuously into a pretty patchwork mosaic best appreciated from the air.

Kathmandu, Patan and Bhaktapur all lie in the lush Kathmandu Valley, in Nepal's Middle Hills. The name Kathmandu is a variant of Kasthamandap, a 10th century temple situated near Durbar Square. Before the unification of the valley under the Shah dynasty, the name referred only to the southern portion of the city; its northern part was called Kantipur, City of Beauty, and the whole city was known locally by its Newari name, Ya. Likewise, Patan was once Lalitpur, the City of Arts, or Yala in Newari, while Bhaktapur, the City of Devotees, is still called Bhadgaon by Gorkhalis, and Khwopa by its Newar residents. Green rice terraces are a beautiful sight, whether near Nagarkot (above) in the Kathmandu Valley or in Rumtek, Sikkim (following pages). Spring turns Nepal's eastern slopes (left) red and white with forests of huge rhododendron trees, while the dry earth of the hillsides indicates that the monsoon rains are due.

Roof of the World

At an average altitude of over 4,000 metres above sea level, and with large portions over 5,000 metres, the Tibetan Plateau does indeed deserve the title Roof of the World. Little of the monsoon is able to cross the Himalayas onto it. Not only is the plateau high and cold, it is also as dry as a desert.

The Karakoram, Kunlun and Altyn mountain ranges bound the plateau to the north and west. Outside the polar caps, this northwest region of Tibet is the most unexplored territory on earth. Temperatures in this landscape of extremes differ as much as 27 degrees Celsius in a single day.

Most of the population live around the few rivers that have managed to struggle across the plateau. This is the source of many of Asia's greatest rivers. The Ganges, Brahmaputra, Yellow River, Mekong, and the Irrawaddy all begin here.

A fine balance is required to live in such a harsh yet fragile landscape, a balance which the inhabitants have successfully struck through the centuries. Tibet's nomads in particular move through this vastness leaving hardly a trace. The plateau is one of our planet's last remaining wilderness areas. The Dalai Lama would like to see Tibet designated a 'zone of peace', to help preserve her delicate ecological balance.

Though its broad expanses are mostly dry, the Tibetan Plateau is nevertheless home to some permanent lakes and small river systems. Surrounding these lakes and rivers, however, are mostly barren deserts and frozen mountains (top right). Tibet's major river, the Yarlung Tsangpo, flows in the south of the country, along the borders with Nepal, India and Bhutan. The river is vital for farming, and irrigates cultivated barley fields like these in Gyantse (top left). Elsewhere, the Tibetan Plateau is little more than rock, dust and snow (above).

A common trait of Ladakh's cliffs are circular strata which show the immense geological forces that thrust up the mountains. In the bleak landscape (right) the only feature is the road snaking through the mountains, drawn as if by the finger of a god, who left the rest of the scene untouched. The path is less clear at the snowy heights of Ladakh's Khardung La (facing page, bottom right). It is one of the highest roads in the world, nearly 5,500 metres above sea level.

The Bridge of Sighs

Northwest of Ladakh is Mount Godwin Austen, or K2. At 8,611 metres above sea level, it is the world's second highest peak. High mountain passes dot Ladakh's lunar landscape. In fact 'Ladakh' translates as 'Land of Many Passes' in the Ladakhi language. In this high landscape many of the vertiginous passes remain snowbound for much of the year.

Formed by water cutting through rock over millions of years, these high and narrow mountain passes were sniffed out by intrepid merchants and travellers who sought access to lands across the Himalayas. Leh, Ladakh's capital, was a major cosmopolitan trading hub along the southern section of the Silk Route linking India, Tibet and Central Asia.

Some of the world's highest roads traverse this mountain region. The ancient trade route from Leh to the Central Asian oasis cities of Yarkand and Kashgar (now in China's Xinjiang Province) took traders through the Karakoram Pass and over the Himalayas at altitudes that made horses and humans bleed profusely from the nose.

Of this tenacious yet beautiful mountain corridor Sven Hedin, who visited Ladakh several times at the end of the 19th century, wrote:

'Like an enormous Bridge of Sighs, it spans with its airy arches the highest mountain land of Asia and of the World.'

RIVERS AND RAIN

The Himalayan region is drained by 19 major rivers, the largest of which are the Indus and Brahmaputra. Centuries of rivers coursing over rock has created deep valleys sandwiched between sheer mountain walls. Spectacular scenery no doubt, but access to the water is difficult. Rain is not predictable either. It depends on location and altitude with respect to the important monsoon winds. Because the Himalayas act as an enormous climatic barrier, monsoon-bearing winds are forced to give up their moisture before crossing onto the Tibetan Plateau. Tibet and Ladakh are therefore dry and arid, while parts of Nepal, Bhutan and Sikkim receive heavy rainfall and snow.

In Nepal children dance with glee as the first huge drops of monsoon rain fall from cloudy skies. Adults raise their faces to the heavens thanking the gods for bringing once more the rains that guarantee a good harvest in the coming year.

A few weeks later heavy rains falling long into the night cause a landslide that dams an already swollen river. The rain continues. The dam finally bursts and a wall of water, rock and mud thunders through a village downstream, carrying away houses, livestock and people.

A few kilometres away, beyond the peaks, a different scene unfolds. Ditches are hacked through bone-dry soil to bring a trickle of water to fields. After meals dishes are licked clean; water is too hard to come by and the dishes will, after all, soon be used again.

Water is scarce in the Himalayas, and its appearance amidst barren rock often hallows the surrounding area. Bhutan's capital in the 17th century was situated at the confluence of the Mo and Po rivers. Today the famous Punakha Dzong (top left) marks this auspicious location. The fertile soils along the banks of the Yarlung Tsangpo River in Shigatse, Tibet, are often carted away by farmers (above) to use as bedding upon which to cultivate barley. To the eye weary of the undulating dryness of the Tibetan Plateau, a refreshing change is the sight of yak skin coracles floating on placid waters (centre right). Waters flow from sacred mountain Ama Dablam (facing page) in the Everest region on the border between Nepal and Tibet. One of the most beautiful mountains of the Himalayas, Ama Dablam takes its name from the small intricate container in which Tibetans carry a statue of the Buddha when they journey about the plateau. The mountain has the significance of being the repository of the Buddha's teachings and waters that flow from it represent the spread of Buddhism.

The Monsoon

Clouds build slowly in the first months of each year over the Bay of Bengal. Around the first of June, the first rains finally sweep in from across the Indian Ocean towards India's southern tip. It takes about two or three more weeks for the monsoon rains to work their way up the subcontinent, before crashing into the Himalayas and unleashing their moisture on the slopes. Suddenly the world is transformed. Baked and cracked khaki-coloured soil gives way to a luscious green. The Middle Hills, dull reddish-brown only a few weeks ago, now shimmer with cascades of luminous green terraces. Hillsides ring with the voices of women and men who are hard at work weeding and fixing the mud terrace walls weakened by the previous night's rains.

The Himalayan summits far above disappear under a dense continent of clouds. The peaks remain almost totally hidden until the rains disperse at the end of September. Sometimes the flank or peak of some mountain will flash for an instant, before being engulfed by the crush of bruising grey clouds.

In the valleys rivers rise and bridges are washed away along with careless cattle and people. Old houses in towns collapse under the strain of continuous downpours. A highway disappears under a lake of cinnamon brown water. People complain, but not too much. The monsoon is a gift of the gods and without it there would be nothing.

Monsoon rains do not stop the buying and selling that take place outside Kasthamandap (above), the temple that gives Kathmandu its name. The Kathmandu Valley is damp between July and October each year, when heavy rain makes life without umbrellas and raincoats impossible (top left). Clear blue skies fill with grey clouds that hang low over a valley of vibrant green rice fields (top right). We might as well be on another planet when we cross over to the other side of the Himalayas. Yulchung village in Zanskar, Ladakh (facing page, top right) sits entombed within dry mountains, while sand dunes in Tsedang, central Tibet (right) are whipped about by fierce, stinging winds devoid of moisture.

In the Rain Shadow

The Himalayas present an almost unbreachable barrier to the monsoon rains. Pokhara, practically bumping the Annapurnas on the southern side of the Himalayas, gets about 3,500 millimetres of rain a year. Less than 50 kilometres away, but on the northern side of the Annapurna Range, Manang gets about 350 millimetres per year. At Leh only 70 to 150 millimetres of rain fall annually. Lhasa in Tibet averages not much more, around 400 millimetres per year.

The rain shadow created north of the Himalayas means vast areas of the Tibetan Plateau have no river systems at all and are, for all practical purposes, desert. Tibet has some lakes that are important breeding grounds for migratory birds. There are also dead lakes here, brackish pools that are probably remnants of the prehistoric Tethys Sea that vanished as the plateau thrust up. Living lakes may vary in size and location from year to year. Some lakes have been known to 'wander' or disappear according to the unreliable amounts of rain and the strong wind.

Much of Tibet's sparse precipitation falls in the form of snow. The runoff from the melting snow feeds the four great holy rivers of the Indian subcontinent: the Ganges, Sutlej, Brahmaputra and Indus, all of which originate around Mount Kailash in the far west of Tibet. Lack of rain, combined with a cold climate, rules out life as a sedentary farmer. Living in the rain shadow compels Tibetans into the nomadic life of herders and traders for which they are well known.

PART TWO
FLORA AND FAUNA

The Himalayan Kingdom supports an astonishing variety of flora and fauna, a reality perhaps somewhat overshadowed by the grandeur of its mountainous landscape. Each ridge soars up from a tropical river valley through three or four climatic zones to a towering peak, only to plunge down the other side. Differences in exposure to sunlight mean that a ridge's north-facing slope supports different ecological systems from its south-facing slope. Annual rainfall decreases dramatically both as you cross northwards through the Himalayas and as you move from east to west. The result is tremendous biodiversity.

A tiger lies concealed in a bamboo grove by a rushing river. Just two kilometres up the same ridge a snow leopard roams the rocky summit, content in its solitude. Nepal contains over 800 species of birds, nearly 10% of known varieties. Bhutan has hundreds and hundreds of orchid species.

Sikkim's proximity to the Bay of Bengal offers direct exposure to the monsoon rains and, coincidentally, the highest incidence of lightning strikes in the world. Lightning induces nitrogen in the soil and improves its fertility, enabling Sikkim to support 4,000 types of flowering plants and shrubs. It is no wonder that Sikkim, blessed with the richest variety of flora in India, has been likened to the biblical Garden of Eden.

Part of this wealth are the more than 450 varieties of orchids that grow within Sikkim's borders. These flowers, in turn, play host to over 600 species of butterfly. Although butterflies traditionally prefer warmer and wetter climates, the attraction extended by the orchids is so entrancing that in Sikkim gaily coloured butterflies flutter right up to 2,500 metres above sea level. Canopies of them swarm in forested valleys, hovering over the equally colourful orchids. Sikkim is also an ornithologist's paradise, being home to several hundred bird species, from the tiny flowerpecker to the bearded vulture, or lammergeier, with its enormous wingspan.

There are a number of lakes in the Chang Thang area of Ladakh, the largest of which is the one hundred kilometre-long Pangong Lake. This lake extends east into remote western Tibet. Among the dozens and dozens of water birds that breed on its banks one species in particular deserves mention: the black-necked crane or Tibetan Crane. Called *cha-thung-thung* by the Ladakhis, the Tibetan Crane is one of only 14 varieties of crane in the world. It is also the least known member of the species.

This great wealth of flora and fauna is coming under increasing threat. Growing human populations destroy jungle habitats to increase agricultural production and cut down forests for cooking fuel. The much publicised plight of the one-horned Asian rhinoceros and the Royal Bengal Tiger are only symptomatic of the pressure entire ecological systems are coming under in the Himalayan regions. The increasingly fragile environmental situation is often the result of people simply trying to improve their own difficult lives. The balance between man and his natural world needs to be struck once more if the tremendous variety of Himalayan flora and fauna is to be preserved.

Himalayan flora and fauna often have religious significance: Flowers such as this yellow poppy (facing page) in northeastern Tibet, or these rhododendrons (facing pages) in central Nepal, are used in worship and are common motifs in the visual arts, while animal horns (above) can sometimes be engraved with Tibetan mantras.

RICHES AND RARITIES

Bhutan's natural habitats are spectacular. Rapidly changing elevation and an annual rainfall of between 50 and 5,500 millimetres produce a wide diversity of flora and fauna. Bhutan has it all, from tropical jungle to arctic desert. The abundance is demonstrated, for example, in Bhutan's 600 species of orchids. There are also plants so rare as to be almost mythical. Bhutan's national flower, the blue poppy, is one such floral jewel.

Bhutan is worthy of special note because of the government's policy to maintain 60% of the land as forest (presently forests cover over 70%). After Sikkim, Bhutan gets the heaviest rainfall in the Himalayas, resulting in an astonishing 5,000 species of plants within its small area. This figure includes more than 300 confirmed medicinal species.

Much larger Nepal has a similar diversity of climatic zones housing over 6,500 identified plant species. With her much faster population growth, Nepal has not been able to maintain its forest cover as well as Bhutan, despite her centralised forest management policy. In fact, deforestation is a problem in many parts of the country. In spite of that, the Middle Hills are awe-inspiring, especially in March and April, when thick rhododendron forests bloom and colour entire hillsides white and red.

Across the Himalayas, in the monsoon rain shadow, lies Tibet, almost desert-like over much of its territory. Vegetation struggles to survive in this low rainfall, high altitude environment. Only in the east does the richness of its vegetation rival that of Nepal, Sikkim and Bhutan, its southerly neighbours in the Himalayas.

Different types of flowers grow at different altitudes in the Himalayas. Daisies and marigolds, like these (facing page, top) at a tourist lodge in western Sikkim, are common at lower altitudes. Households take pride in cultivating their gardens (facing page, centre and bottom). This garden (above) in Choglamat, Ladakh, supplies vegetables and herbs, both of which are rare and valuable in the high, dry climate. The garden is tended by children, whose diligent work has made it thrive amidst barren mountains. The following pages reveal the wealth of plant life found throughout the length and breadth of the Himalayas.

The Orchid Paradise

The monsoon blesses the slopes of the Himalayas just as equally as it does India's rice fields to the south. Among those blessings are over 600 species of orchids identified in both Sikkim and Bhutan. Further to the west, slightly drier Nepal has over 500 species. Isolation and adaptation are the key reasons for this diversity. Steep slopes start in low tropical river valleys and vault up to alpine meadows at 4,000 metres above sea level. These are ideal conditions for creating unique subspecies of orchids adapted specifically for the small local climate enclosed by those high slopes. The aspect of the slope with regard to the sun and the direction of the winds also play a significant part in determining the many variations that occur here within the orchid species.

The orchid's usual habitat is low-lying tropical jungle, but in Bhutan many species grow up to 2,100 metres above sea level, and some species have even been located at 3,700 metres. Orchids in general need heat and rain. Although temperature drops as altitude increases, on south-facing slopes the sun's intensity actually rises with altitude. Rainfall also increases with altitudes up to a height of 2,700 metres above sea level. These conditions increase the chance for a new subspecies to evolve, especially when the high slopes above the tree line keep most kinds of intruders out.

Even at the ripe old age of 101 years, this Skkimese Brahmin woman (above) still enjoys tending her orchids in Rumtek, Sikkim. The Himalayas support an incredible number of orchid species (left, right and below). Orchids are not the only exotic flowers in these mountains. The rare blue poppy (facing page) is the national flower of Bhutan, and other members of the poppy family (top left) are also found in the region.

Symbol of a Nation

It was discovered by botanists less than 70 years ago and its reclusive nature is a good metaphor for the country that has adopted it as the national flower. Its toughness and fondness for high places also captures the national character. Bhutan's Blue Poppy, or *euitgel metog hoem* in Bhutan's Dzongkha language, is indeed a flower to be proud of.

The Blue Poppy is only found above the tree line at altitudes of between 3,500 to 4,500 metres. Such high places exist all over Bhutan, from the eastern border right across to the western frontiers. In these high regions it grows to a height of over a metre, taking several years before it blooms. A monocarpic plant, the Blue Poppy blooms once, and then dies at the apex of its life. It blooms from late May to July, at the peak of the monsoon.

Its inaccessibility due to high altitude and high rainfall explains why the flower eluded western discovery until 1933, when British botanist George Sherriff classified it for the first time. He chanced upon a specimen on a rugged pass in a remote section of eastern Bhutan. Until then the flower was probably regarded as a myth, like the yeti. Now, however, its existence has been confirmed, but the chances of ever seeing one blossom in the wild are very slim indeed.

SPIRITUAL ANCHORS

The duck (above) this boy carries will be sacrificed in a few minutes at the famous temple of Dakshinkali near Kathmandu. It then becomes part of the family's picnic lunch. Sheep and goat (facing page, top left and right) are an important feature of the Himalayan landscape and provide wool, which is then spun into blankets, clothes and carpets (facing page, bottom).

Domesticated animals are important partners in the life of the Himalayan people. They represent sources of labour, food, fuel, clothes and building material, and are even a focus of worship; they make life possible in this difficult environment. Wealth in the Himalayas is often linked to the number of animals owned by a family.

Sheep are important to the hill tribes and are used, just like mules and donkeys, as beasts of burden. It is not unusual to see great herds of them moving down a trail with a small pair of bags straddling their backs.

Yaks are so important to Tibetans that each yak is given its own name, no matter how large the herd. Buddhist Tibetans and Bhutanese will not slaughter yaks although they have no qualms about eating their meat.

To Hindus cows are much more than a resource; they are the reincarnation of gods. As such they can bestow blessings through mere touch. To harm them is to ensure certain punishment — an inferior rebirth of the soul's future reincarnation.

Animals are not only valuable resources. They are spiritual anchors in this rugged landscape guiding the Himalayan people through their equally rugged lives.

Yaks, mules and horses are perhaps the most common pack animals in the Himalayan Kingdom. All three are also used to plough fields. A mule (top right) helps his master plough in central Tibet. Yaks (above), the lifeblood of Himalayan traders, traverse the Himalayas near Zemathang, Sikkim, while a horse caravan (left) crosses a river en route to Mount Chomolhari, via the 7,350-metre high Phajoding Pass in Bhutan. Crossing streams and rivers is hazardous, especially in the monsoon season when small streams turn into raging torrents.

The Yak

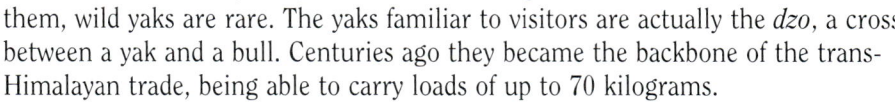

Central to life in the Himalayas is the yak. In the wilds of Ladakh the yak can reach a height of nearly two metres at the shoulder, weigh over a ton, and sport horns more than a metre across. Top all this off with a great shaggy coat that hangs to the ground and the yak is a truly impressive sight.

Great yak herds once roamed all over the Tibetan plateau. Today, despite a ban on hunting them, wild yaks are rare. The yaks familiar to visitors are actually the *dzo*, a cross between a yak and a bull. Centuries ago they became the backbone of the trans-Himalayan trade, being able to carry loads of up to 70 kilograms.

Their value does not end there. Yak's wool is used to make everything from the sacks they carry on their backs to Santa Claus beards in America and wigs for Kabuki and Noh drama in Japan. Their tails are used in rites by both Hindus and Buddhists. Yaks are the main source of milk and butter in the Himalayas. They are also a valuable source of meat. Dried yak dung has its use too as fuel for fire.

Yaks are well suited to high altitudes as they have an extra pair or two of ribs and more red blood cells than lowland cattle. Both make for easier breathing at high altitudes. They are remarkably surefooted, even graceful, on mountain trails, and their huge square tongues and broad muzzles help root up snow and soil for grass.

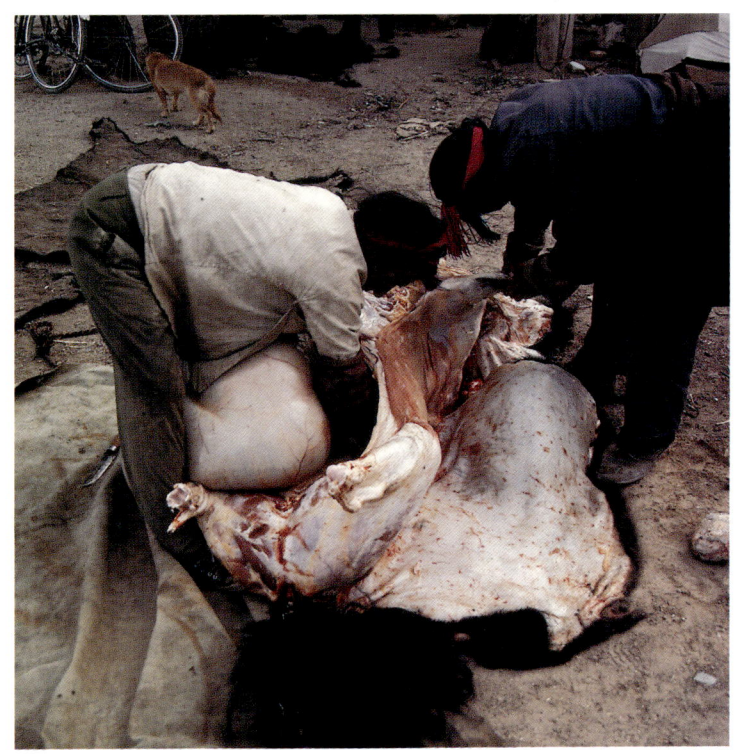

Many yaks are actually a cross between bulls and yaks. True yaks can be huge, bigger than these domesticated examples in Tibet's Nenang Valley (facing page, top left), and Bhutan's Thongbula Shong Pass (facing page, top right). Yak meat and hides are taken to Lhasa by Muslim Hui traders (top right), who sell them at Lhasa's Barkhor Market (below). The yak butter here (centre right) is sold in an inverted yak torso. Khampa men slaughter a yak near Drepung Monastery in Tibet (left). Yaks graze peacefully (facing page, bottom) on pastures between Amdo and Lhasa in Tibet.

A Sacred Beast

Cows in the Hindu religion are the earthly incarnation of Lakshmi, wife of Vishnu and Goddess of Wealth. They provide the essentials of both life and worship: milk, yogurt, butter and dung. Krishna started life as a cowherd and milk remained his favourite food. Milk is also poured over the phallic Shiva *lingams* in Hindu *pujas*, or rites. All parts of a cow are sacred. Even its urine is believed to be medicinal while cow dung is a source of fuel.

To die while holding a cow's tail is believed to make the soul's journey through the underworld quick and easy. Each August in the Kathmandu Valley, during Gai Jatra or the Cow Festival, cows or small boys dressed as cows are led through the street, in the belief that the newly deceased can grab a tail and pass on safely into the underworld.

The third day of the Tihar Festival is when Lakshmi visits each home. Cows are washed and their horns painted. They are further sprinkled with red powder and garlanded with flowers. People touch their forehead to the cow's body and kneel at their feet. A cow's life, however, is not all paradise. In any bazaar a cow can be rapped on the muzzle with a heavy stick for stealing vegetables even as a passerby bends his forehead to the cow's flank for a blessing.

Cows are revered in Nepal because they are considered the incarnation of the gods. This statue of a cow (top left) is incredibly lifelike, with its brightly painted yellow and red horns and fresh garlands of flowers. Cows take full advantage of their sacred status to raid unprotected fields as well as food stands in urban areas. This cow (above) at Jana Bahal Temple in Kathmandu, Nepal, is looking for its chance. Bullock carts are a common sight in Nepal's Terai region (top right), moving people, hay and grain across its flat expanse.

BIRDS OF THE HEIGHTS

More than 800 species of birds, almost 10% of all known species in the world, have been identified within Nepal's borders. The same climatic wealth that leads to a multitude of plant species also nourishes a large variety of birds. Many of the birds here are migratory, spending summers north of the Himalayas and crossing south in the winter. The comical bar-headed goose has been observed flying across the Himalayas at an altitude of 8,000 metres above sea level. The rare and endangered black-necked crane arrives in Bhutan each fall after breeding in Ladakh and Tibet.

There are 17 species of cuckoo in Nepal, each with its own distinct call. Perhaps the most famous call is that of the hawk cuckoo. Its repetitive and gradually deafening version has earned it the nickname 'brain fever' bird, after the excruciating malarial fever endured by British *sahibs*, or army officers, in the past.

The Himalayas are also home to several species of vulture, the largest being the lammergeier, or bearded vulture, who has one of the largest wingspans of any bird — over three metres. These now endangered birds soar across the mountains, building their nests in inaccessible crags and niches.

Sky Burial

In Tibet vultures perform a unique service. Cremation is rendered impractical because of the lack of fuel wood, while burial is impossible due to the hard, frozen ground. Enter the vulture, who assists Tibetans in disposing of their corpses by a unique means called 'sky burial'. The body is carried to a high place designated for burials. Special people called *rogyapa* cut up the body into pieces, pound the bones together with *tsampa*, or barley, and leave the resulting preparation for the vultures to eat. Since the soul is considered to have already departed and entered a new body, this 'sky burial' is merely the disposal of a useless corpse.

The Himalayas boast many species of birds, that live in different habitats at different altitudes. The green bee eater (top right) inhabits a wide area between the hills of Sikkim and the flat Ganges River delta of the Sundarbans in Bangladesh to the south. The calm shores of Pangong Lake (above), which straddles Tibet and Ladakh, belie the fact that it is an important breeding ground for dozens of bird species. They flock here in their hundreds during the breeding season. Predators loom large in the Himalayan Kingdom: vultures (left) dispose of human corpses in Tibet, while their relative, the common buzzard (top left), stalks the southern Himalayan slopes.

THE INEVITABLE CONFLICT

The beauty and variety of Himalayan animal and plant life is not without its challenges. In areas of high population growth the clash between wildlife and people is inevitable. Elephants and rhinoceroses devour fields that were once part of their jungle. Leopards and tigers prey on livestock where deer previously grazed. Monkeys consume between a fifth and a third of a farmer's average yield. These conflicts usually end in the death of the animals.

At night rhinos still plunder fields across the river from Chitwan National Park in Nepal. Farmers waving fiery torches chase them back into the reserve. Next morning the very same rhinos will be on display for elephant-mounted tourists, the latter having paid more for their short exotic safari than the farmers will earn in a year.

Bhutan's Buddhist code forbids killing, but loss of habitat either for fields or timber puts endangered species like the red panda, the wild buffalo and the hornbill at even greater risk. The same is true of the wild yak in Ladakh.

Selling tiger and snow leopard skins is illegal, but still happens in certain fur shops. Musk deer, tiger and Himalayan black bear are all prized for the medicinal power their body parts supposedly possess. Western conservation beliefs mean little to a farmer when a marauding rhinoceros consumes his crop. An illegal hunter may have no idea of the real value, either intrinsic or monetary, of the game he sells for a pittance to an unscrupulous middleman.

Animal trophies from today and yesterday: Lepcha hunters descend upon their hapless victim (below), a civet cat, in northern Sikkim. Economics is important to this man in Tibet (above), who can make good money as a middleman for skins from tigers slaughtered in Nepal and India, and then sold in the Chinese market. Members of Nepal's ancient Rana clan (bottom left and right) pose by their kills.

Tiger! Tiger! Burning Bright

Grandest of the big cats, the Royal Bengal Tiger is found in both Nepal and Bhutan. It grows to 3 metres in length inclusive of tail and can weigh more than 250 kilograms. They are truly magnificent animals. Their usual habitat is the thick jungle, grassland or swamp, where their beautiful black-striped orange coat gives effective camouflage.

Males may need about 100 square kilometres of territory in which to roam. Their turf can also sustain two or three females. Tigers feed on the several types of Himalayan deer. Sometimes cattle, and on rare occasions people, also fall victim to them. Bhutan's Royal Manas and Jigme Dori National Parks and Nepal's Royal Chitwan and Royal Bardia National Parks all have a tiger population.

Although they prefer the lowlands, tigers are sometimes reported at higher elevations in both Nepal and Bhutan. The steep valleys of the Middle Hills provide thick cover along low-lying rivers, from which tigers can travel uphill in search of prey.

The Rhinoceros

The one-horned Asian rhinoceros is the largest of the three rhinoceros species found in Asia, and is a genus distinct from the African rhinoceros. All rhinoceros species are endangered. Four of the five species are nearly extinct and the one-horned Asian rhinoceros now exists only in Nepal, and in Sikkim and Assam in India.

Standing nearly two metres tall at the shoulder and weighing up to two thousand kilograms, rhinoceroses are survivors of a prehistoric age. Their thick, extremely tough hide is marked by folds at the neck and limb joints, giving them the appearance of being encased in armour.

Rhinos are notorious for their poor eyesight. However, their amazingly acute sense of smell and hearing more than make up for it. While they have the bulk of a truck they also have the speed and agility of a well-tuned sports car.

Normally they are timid and peaceful, but they can charge with devastating speed and force when threatened, especially a female rhinoceros guarding her young.

Their distinctive horn, the cause of much of their slaughter, is a mass of agglutinated keratin, the protein found in hair. The rhinoceros uses it for digging up the bulbs, grasses and other vegetation on which it feeds.

Rhinoceroses draw thousands of tourists to Royal Chitwan National Park (above and left), making it Nepal's second most popular tourist destination after Kathmandu. Valuable jobs are created by Nepal's vibrant tourist industry and the money earned is pumped back into the local economy. But the national conservation parks draw mixed reactions from the neighbouring farmers, who frequently have to put up with escaped animals that eat their crops and destroy their property. A magnificent Royal Bengal Tiger (top left) suspiciously eyes the camera while swimming up a murky stream in Chitwan, Nepal.

OF REALITY AND MYTH

The seasonal settlement of Macchermo is situated high in the Mount Everest region. In 1974 a young woman there was grazing her yaks when she heard a roar as something knocked her unconscious. She awoke to find her yaks dead, their necks snapped. Yeti? Bear? For many people it was a yeti, plain and simple.

Animals hold a powerful place in the Himalayas. Mythical creatures like the yeti are sworn to exist. Rare creatures of beauty like the snow leopard are hunted to the point of extinction. The monkey is an insufferable pest to farmers. Yet Hanuman, the strong, loyal Monkey King of the *Ramayana*, remains one of every Hindu's favourite heroes. When Hanuman could not remember which herbs to collect that would help his wounded friends, he simply lifted the whole mountain and carried it to them on his back.

The Bhutanese call their kingdom Druk Yul, or Land of the Thunder Dragon, and themselves Drukpa, or people of the Thunder Dragon. To see storm clouds rear up and out of a steep Druk Yul valley answers any questions about the name. Dragons are also a favourite subject for Tibet's carpet weavers. So too is the fierce snow lion, with its billowing white mane. Do they exist? Are they another myth? In the Himalayas the line between myth and reality is hard to draw, but there are a few who are anyway inclined to draw it.

Hanuman, the Monkey King (above), sets fire to Lanka, city of the demon king Ravana, after being caught spying for Lord Ram. Another figure with animal symbolism is elephant-headed Ganesh (facing page, top right), the remover of all obstacles and the first god invoked at the start of prayers. He likes to dance and is often depicted in a jaunty pose. In Hindu religion Brahma (facing page, top left), the supreme power and ultimate reality of the universe, has a mythical 'hamsa' bird for a mount. The snow leopard (bottom left) is not a mythical creature, but its declining numbers have made it a rare one indeed.

Sir Edmund Hillary, conqueror of Everest, returned to Nepal in 1960 to investigate the mystery of the yeti. Here he stands (right) with Khunjo Chumbi, the Sherpa entrusted with what was purported to be a yeti scalp. Khumjung Monastery, where the scalp was kept, permitted Hillary to take it out of Nepal on condition that Chumbi accompanied it and that it would be returned within a month. Analysis of the scalp in Chicago found it to be from a Himalayan goat. It is shaped like a priest's cap with coarse reddish-black hair, and is believed to be more than 100 years old.

The Abominable Snowman

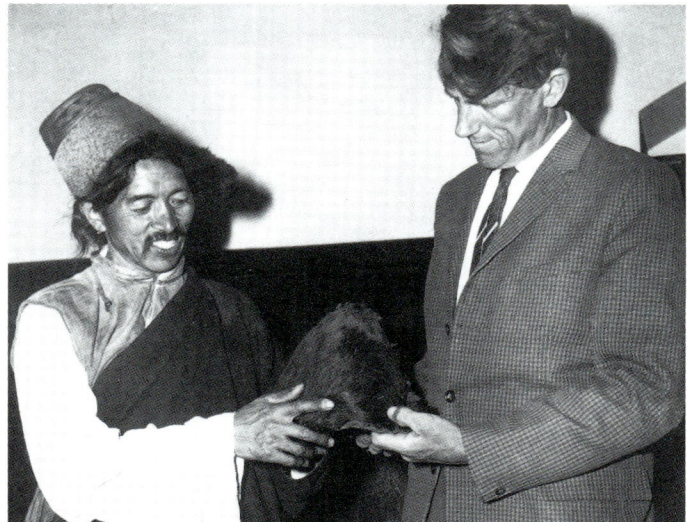

Adding to the timeless myths of the mountains is the story of the abominable snowman, called the *yeti* in Nepal, *migoi* in Bhutan, *migyu* in Tibet, and *neeguyed* in Sikkim.

Descriptions of the snowman vary from place to place. The Sherpas who share their mountains with the yeti describe three types: a huge cattle-eating creature over two metres tall, a much smaller apelike beast, and a man-sized snowman with a human face and a shaggy coat of red hair.

In Bhutan the yeti's hair colour varies from red to black and the feet face backwards, a trait also heard of in Nepal. Another characteristic attributed to the snowman — this one shared all across the Himalayas — is its overpowering bad smell. The Bhutanese snowman apparently avoids capture by its special ability to become invisible.

In 1960 Edmund Hillary found supposed yeti skins and a legendary yeti scalp in Khumjung Monastery in the Mount Everest area. Scientific analysis determined the items to be from known Tibetan animals such as the blue bear and Himalayan goat. This did not, however, spell the end of the legend. Bhutan has gone so far as to set aside the Sakteng Wildlife Sanctuary as a likely yeti habitat. Reinhold Messner, the first man to climb Mount Everest unaccompanied, is sure the yeti exists and is determined to find one. The mystery continues to haunt the Himalayas, and is renewed and embellished under tents and around camp fires.

The Snow Leopard

As rare as the abominable snowman, but proven to exist, is the snow leopard, the largest Himalayan predator. It prowls the rocky cliffs at an average of 4,500 metres above sea level, going higher in summer in pursuit of its favourite prey, *thar* and *serow*, both species of wild Himalayan goat.

These beautiful cats are undeniably elegant. With a sleek frame over a metre long, their presence is enhanced by an equally long and magnificent bushy tail. The coat of the snow leopard is a lustrous pearl grey spotted with black rosettes. A black band running down the length of its spine completes the luxurious ensemble.

Shy, solitary and nocturnal, the snow leopard prefers steep cliffs and will relocate if it feels threatened by competition from other predators. An endangered species, their solitary nature does not lend itself to breeding in captivity. They have been hunted so rapaciously for their beautiful coat that their continued existence is sometimes in doubt.

Animal Symbolism

King of the Drukpa, or Dragon People, the Bhutanese monarch wears the Raven Crown, symbol of Mahakala, the protecting deity of the first king who unified Bhutan. The lion is the symbol of Nepal's king. In Nepalese art Vishnu is depicted as a lion, a boar, a fish or a tortoise. Included in Tibet's eight auspicious symbols are the Golden Fish, a pair of fish leaping from the waters of captivity to symbolize freedom from the Wheel of Life.

The Wind Horse of Tibet carries to heaven the three jewels of Buddhism: the Buddha, the *dharma*, or law, and the *sangha*, or monastic community. Ananta, the eleven-headed King of the *Naga*, or Cobras, carries Vishnu on a bed formed by his own huge coils as they both float in the cosmic ocean.

Each of the Hindu gods and goddesses has their own mount, an animal they ride. Ganesh, the popular roly-poly elephant-headed son of Shiva and patron of writers and thieves, rides a mouse. Shiva himself rides a bull, and Lakshmi, Goddess of Wealth, circles the globe on her white owl. Garuda, the half eagle-half human mount of Vishnu is regarded in Tibetan Buddhism as a malevolent force. Shri Devi, the Buddhist deity who protects both Lhasa and the Dalai Lama's Gelukpa order, rides a mule which has a third eye in its rump. Similarly, the Hindu goddess Durga sits astride her tiger as she battles a demon disguised as a great water buffalo.

*D*ragons and lions are popular motifs in the Himalayan Kingdom: A carved lion (above) looks down at the city of Lhasa from the 13th floor of the Potala Palace in Tibet; a gigantic dragon (centre left) faces snow-capped mountains at Yaksha Resort in Lachung, northern Sikkim. Exterior walls of the houses (left) of the Tharu tribe in Nepal's Terai region are often decorated with animal paintings. These act as charms protecting the dwellings from harm and increasing the livestock of the household. Mythical animals, cascading from each other's mouths (centre right), adorn a stone water spout near Bajra Jogini Temple in Sankhu, Nepal.

On the roof of Lo Manthang Palace in Mustang, Nepal, horns of various animals (facing page) are piled high in a pyramid to bring good luck. Sculptures of deer (top left) flank the Dharma Wheel, their attentive poses showing the respect that even animals give to the teachings of the Buddha. Punakha Dzong (above) in Bhutan decorates its walls with a menagerie of animals. They each symbolise a human vice or virtue in Buddhist artistic iconography. The pair of Bhutanese golden fish (top right) represent the soul's ability to swim freely once liberated by faith, while the golden yak (centre right) in Lhasa was erected by the Chinese government as a monument to the 'peaceful liberation' of Tibet.

PART THREE
PEOPLE, CUSTOMS AND BELIEFS

From early morning the entrance of the Jokhang, Lhasa's holiest shrine, is crowded with worshippers and pilgrims. They prostrate themselves on cold paving stones worn smooth as glass from centuries of such practice.

On a foggy winter morning in Kathmandu women and children, wrapped in shawls against the dawn chill, carry trays of red powder, fruit, sweets, flowers and incense to the neighbourhood temple, there to offer this bounty in worship. Others are on their way home already, their trays full of *prasad*: the blessing of fruit, sweets, and flowers from the temple, which will be distributed to everyone at home. They pass a shopkeeper who, before opening for business, makes an offering to the picture of Lakshmi, Goddess of Wealth, that hangs on the wall, garlanded in flowers. Back home, there is a puja room on the roof, from which the sounds of bells ringing float down as worshippers alert the gods to their prayers and beseech them to accept their offerings.

In rural Bhutan wives refresh the water in seven silver bowls and light the butter lamps that stand on the family altar. Above the altar hangs a portrait of the Buddha draped in *kata*, the pure white scarf used as an offering. Old villagers gather in the warming morning sun to gossip or doze. Some spin in their hands a prayer wheel with a mantra written inside it. Every revolution completes a prayer. In this way prayer wheels fly millions of prayers up to the heavens each morning all across the Himalayas.

High on a ridge in the Himalayas herders graze their yaks, prayer beads clasped in hand. Mantras rumble from deep inside their chests. Each time they complete the mantra their thumbs flick a prayer bead forward. At a pass they pause to tie prayer flags to the strings of flags already there. The string is released and the flags flutter in the wind. Each flutter sends the prayer heavenward.

On the road to Pokhara, Nepal, a bus hurtles around a narrow bend. On the dashboard is a picture of Shiva. The fresh garlands around the picture swing with the rocking of the bus. Suddenly the driver slams to a stop, jumps out, and runs into a small structure. Moments later he emerges and races back to the bus, watched by the priest of this tiny temple. He hops back into his seat, his forehead red with the powder with which the priest has anointed him. Within moments the bus is speeding away again.

Throughout the Himalayas the threads of worship and faith are woven with those of daily life into a seamless, living fabric. For centuries people have started each day appealing to the Buddha or the hundreds of Hindu gods. Throughout the day they blend acts of faith with the life's mundane moments. Faith, embraced at each turn, is the source of strength in the difficult lives of most Himalayan people.

Women of the Himalayas: A lady pilgrim (facing page) worships the Buddha contained behind the locked doors of a chorten in Thimphu, Bhutan; a Nepalese lady (above), a member of the Thakali ethnic group famous for their skill as hoteliers and cooks, offers apples for sale to people passing her restaurant in Marpha, Nepal.

TOLERANT WORLD

Muktinath lies far up the valley of the Kali-Gandaki River in central Nepal. Here a small Buddhist shrine sits next to a Hindu temple. Long ago Brahma, the Hindu Creator of the Universe, visited Muktinath and as an act of worship created a flame on the waters of a nearby lake. The flame still burns today beneath a rock altar. Hindus have made pilgrimages to Muktinath for thousands of years. The temple of Vishnu is also visited by Buddhists, who consider the image of Vishnu here a portrayal of Avalokiteshvara, the Bodhisattva of All-Encompassing Compassion. Hindus have long considered Buddha to be the eighth reincarnation of Vishnu. Such open intermingling of the faiths is rare. It is only in urban areas that various ethnic and religious groups find themselves living side by side. Rural villages are usually all of one faith or ethnic group. Muktinath, though, is symbolic of the tolerance that every group, religious or ethnic, has for each other.

Tolerance, however, does not mean uniformity, for Buddhists and Hindus do almost everything differently. Take tea, for example: Tibetans add butter and salt to theirs while Hindus prefer sugar and milk. Over the course of history, tolerant human relationships have been forged against the backdrop of an intolerant natural world. And by no means can this tolerance be taken for granted.

The varied faces of the Himalayan people (this and facing pages) show a mixture of the two main racial groups: Indo-European and Mongol. The Newar men relaxing on a verandah in Thimi, central Nepal (above), are the main ethnic group in the Kathmandu Valley. Whether Buddhist or Hindu, Newars in practice often adopt whichever religious custom seems appropriate at the time; both groups are aware of each other's traditions. Gaines (bottom left) are a musician caste from a village near Pokhara, and once roamed the Nepalese countryside entertaining people with accounts of Nepal's myths and history. Today the radio, television, cinema and video have all led to their decline.

A TEST OF FAITH

Life is hard no matter where you live in the Himalayas. Regions sharing this mountain system usually rank near the bottom of economic indices. Bhutan has an annual per capita income of about US$500, Nepal less than half that. Tibet remains one of the poorest areas in the region while Ladakh and Sikkim are among the least developed of Indian states.

Subsistence agriculture and animal husbandry are the major means of livelihood for the majority of people. A bad harvest, a monsoon flood or a freak hailstorm can destroy crops and ruin a family for years. The particularly severe winter of 1997–98 killed off more than one-fifth of livestock in the Naqu region of Tibet, devastating herding families there. In the mid 1980s a fierce monsoon storm washed away a bridge on the main road to Kathmandu, cutting off the city for days.

Electricity is just starting to reach the hills while education is a dream for many, particularly girls. The nearest hospital could be days away on foot. In the Middle Hills it is not unusual to see an invalid being carried on someone's back — stuffed into a woven basket, legs dangling over the rim. Roads are almost nonexistent. Most goods still move across the hills transported either by humans or animals. Daily life in the Himalayan Kingdom is truly a test of faith.

Himalayan women and children bear the brunt of daily chores, be it is gathering firewood or fetching water. Bringing home firewood is typically a woman's job. They start as children accompanying their mothers and grandmothers (below) and continue until they too become elderly grandmothers themselves (far right).

Fetching water is usually a child's task. In rural areas children (top left) have to walk long distances morning and evening to reach water sources. With such demands on children, their school education suffers. The boy monks (left), who must study alongside their daily duties, are lucky. Less lucky are these youngsters (right) selling their fruit on the main thoroughfare in Kathmandu, Nepal. They may have walked hours before dawn to claim this patch of pavement. Taking the bus and paying the fare would eat up the amount they earn from their sales.

A Farmer's Life

About 90% of the Himalayan population depends on subsistence agriculture for a living. Farmers produce enough to feed their families and perhaps a little extra to sell for cash.

Altitude determines which kinds of crops can be grown and where. Rice can grow up to about 2,000 metres; wheat, corn and millet are cultivated up to 8,000 metres beyond that; while barley, buckwheat and potatoes are staples at higher levels.

In the 1970s the clearing of the Terai significantly enlarged the farming belt, and new seeds and farming techniques helped turn Nepal into a rice exporter. Population growth, however, quickly cancelled out the gains. Nepal is today a net importer of grain.

Farming in the Himalayan Kingdom is an arduous task. Terraces have to be built before crops can be planted. These cultivated terraces then need constant care, and are built up and repaired continuously over time. Modern equipment, seeds and fertilisers are beyond the reach of most farmers here and bullock-drawn wooden ploughs are still the norm. A good harvest depends on a farmer's own seed, shared labour and a benevolent monsoon. The failure of any of these can spell disaster.

Shimmering terraces cascading hundreds of metres down a steep hillside are a beautiful sight. Few visitors realise the backbreaking work that goes into cultivating and maintaining these timeless structures, so painstakingly carved into the Himalayan landscape.

*F*arming is a collective task in the Himalayas. Whether ploughing terraces in Sikkim (centre left), or transplanting and harvesting rice in Nepal (previous and facing pages), cooperatives share their labour among members. Courtyards and verandahs (right and top left) are used for the drying of hay and grain, as in rural Bhaktapur, Nepal (above), where women spread grain to dry in the sun.

Moving On

With desert conditions at high altitudes across wide sweeps of the Himalayas there is precious little to tie many Tibetans down to a piece of land. To survive, people have to move on. Whole families move with their herds of yak and sheep. Home is a tent made of yak hide, warmed by a fire, fuelled in turn by the herd's dried dung. The animals provide milk and meat for food, wool for clothes, and leather for bags and shoes. Selling part of the herd provides cash when needed.

Nomadic traders also use their animals to transport goods. The nomad drives his herd of yak or sheep to the lowlands, the animals loaded with salt, skins or wool. As night falls, camp is pitched. Food is prepared and a simple meal eaten. Fierce dogs curl near the crackling fire. From restless yaks comes the sound of clanging neck bells. Sheep bleat while a stream close by cascades down steep slopes. Above, high ridges and snowy peaks frame a night sky studded with diamond-bright stars.

Reaching the lowland markets a few days, weeks or months later, the nomad trades his goods for rice, corn and wheat. The caravan heads home again, selling the grain at markets along the way. The home stay is brief, just long enough to ensure things are well with the wife, the fields, the children. All too soon it is time to move on again.

The Gurkhas

One of Nepal's most enduring images is that of the Gurkha soldier. He is possibly the most famous mercenary in the world, renowned for his physical endurance, bravery and unswerving discipline.

The Gurkhas were originally the elite fighters of the Shah Kingdom of Gorkha in the Middle Hills of Nepal, hence the term 'gurkha'. In the early 19th century war between Nepal and Britain, the British were so impressed by the Gurkhas' fighting ability and indomitable spirit that they immediately recruited the hill warriors for the British army. The Middle Hills have always suffered a shortage of food. So for the men of the hills — the Rai, the Limbu and the Gurung — military service in the British Empire, with its attendant pension, provided for their families in a way farming could not.

Although the British Gurkha contingent is now greatly reduced, particularly after the return of Hong Kong to China, the Gurkhas' contribution to the economy is still important. A contingent now serves as the bodyguard to the Sultan of Brunei.

Getting into the Gurkhas is tough, with thousands competing for few places. The race above is part of the tryout. Recruiting camps take place across Nepal each year. Passing a written test is also a must. Success is rewarded with the colours proudly worn by these soldiers on duty at Hile, Nepal (left).

*N*omads depend on their animals for everything: A family cooks yak meat in their yak hide tent in Peiku Tso, western Tibet (facing page, top right). Sherpa women can sometimes take to the road for pilgrimage, like these women in western Sikkim (left). Nomads sell wherever they find a customer. These Tibetans (bottom centre) have set up a makeshift market by their vehicle to barter their wool. They can work out the value of wool to rice or salt in an instant. In Nepal's remote Nar Valley nomads depend on sheep and goat, which each night have to be carefully counted and herded into pens (bottom left). The toll on the body of a lifetime in the harsh elements and high altitudes is shown on this nomad (below) as he poses proudly in the wind by his tent in western Tibet.

*B*ut a nomad's life is not all work and no play, and horse racing festivals form part of the fun and excitement of plateau life. These horses (facing page, centre) walk past a line of colourful festival tents. Horses are an integral part of life on the broad expanses of the Tibetan Plateau. Boys learn to walk and ride at the same time. Skill on a horse is useful for everything from rounding up yaks to catching the eye of a potential wife. This Bhutanese horseman (top left) smiles happily as he takes a rest on Jimie Langtsho Pass at 3,850 metres above sea level.

Himalayan Bazaar

The Newars, the traditional inhabitants of Kathmandu Valley, are also its traditional merchants. They have shops all across Nepal and far beyond. Newar shops have been in Lhasa for centuries, since the establishment there of Buddhism.

Himalayan bazaars are a colourful affair. Narrow streets are lined with tiny shops in front of which sprawl vendors. One shop sells nothing but kerosene lanterns. A woman squats in front hawking two piles: one of garlic and one of hot chilli peppers. The shop selling cloth is next to the tailor's, while the butcher's is next to the one selling cooking pots. A small boy sells plastic bags on the road. Each is content with his or her own small monopoly. The shopkeeper may be a ten-year-old minding the store while his parents are away having a meal or running errands. Do not expect an easy deal though, for children can be as ruthless as any adult

Many shops appear on the street each morning and disappear each night, carried home on the seller's back. The next morning they reappear in time for the first customers who pass through the bazaar.

Caravanserai

The Ladakhi capital, Leh, was an important link along the southern Silk Road, whose main route led from Xi'an in China to Antioch in the Levant.

An important branch of this main route took the traveller south to Leh over the eastern Karakoram Range. The Ladakhi *serai* referred to the inns at which merchants and their caravans were accommodated by cities along the Silk Road.

In its heyday, Leh had the largest serai south of the main Silk Road, stocking commodities from China such as silk, rugs and tea, and Indian products like cotton, cloth, dyes and coarse sugar. During colonial rule, the British government built and maintained these serais for the convenience of Central Asian caravan traders.

The inns themselves were as important as the bazaar in the main street in town. In fact, the rarer, more exotic products were more likely to be found in the security of the serais than in the chaotic bazaars.

*F*ruits and flowers (left and right) are a feature of most Himalayan bazaars. Bazaars sell anything and everything, from dried cheese in Gangtok's Lal (red) Bazaar (facing page, top right), to colourful jewellery and toys at Kathmandu's Indra Chowk Bazaar (centre right and facing page, centre left), to tin crockery and cutlery in Narayanghat's bazaar in Nepal's Terai region (bottom right). Bazaars are usually a mixture of shops lining the road, hawkers squatting in the street and colourful stalls set up in open squares. Below is an overhead view of the vegetable market in Gangtok, Sikkim.

ANCIENT BELIEFS

Many sects grew up around the teachings of the great Buddhist saints who wandered the vast Tibetan Plateau and the steep Himalayan slopes. Red hats, yellow hats, black hats, these various sects vied for temporal and spiritual power. Eventually the yellow hat Gelukpa sect of the Dalai Lama came to dominate, but the other sects still exist today.

Bhutan, isolated within its natural castle of high peaks, developed Drukpa Kagyu, one of the most Tantric of Buddhist doctrines. It emphasises the power of rituals and meditative tools such as mantras and mandalas to attain enlightenment.

Hinduism is unique among the world's great religions in that it has no organised authority. Hinduism encompasses so vast a multitude of gods, goddesses and beliefs, that a central authority seems neither possible nor desirable. The most visible structure Hinduism has developed is the system of castes, of which the central idea is that one remains throughout one's life in the same social station into which one is born.

Hinduism and Buddhism teach that ego, desire, jealousy and envy are bad. Tolerance is basic to both faiths, and a way to gain merit towards a higher rebirth in the next life. Buddhists and Hindus both believe that only goodness in thought and deed can release us from the cycle of life, death and rebirth to which we are all captive.

Buddhists and Hindus share Swayambhunath, a sacred site in Nepal. At its Hindu temple (below) to Sarasvati, Goddess of Learning, schoolchildren write their names on the walls, hoping for her blessing. At the nearby Buddhist stupa, a monk (facing page) holds up his begging bowl, the symbol of Buddha. In Tibet, pilgrims pray at Jokhang Temple, Lhasa (bottom left), and Tashilunpho Monastery, Shigatse (bottom right), hoping to increase karma. Guiding lay people in spirituality are monks, these of the Gelukpa sect (above and far right).

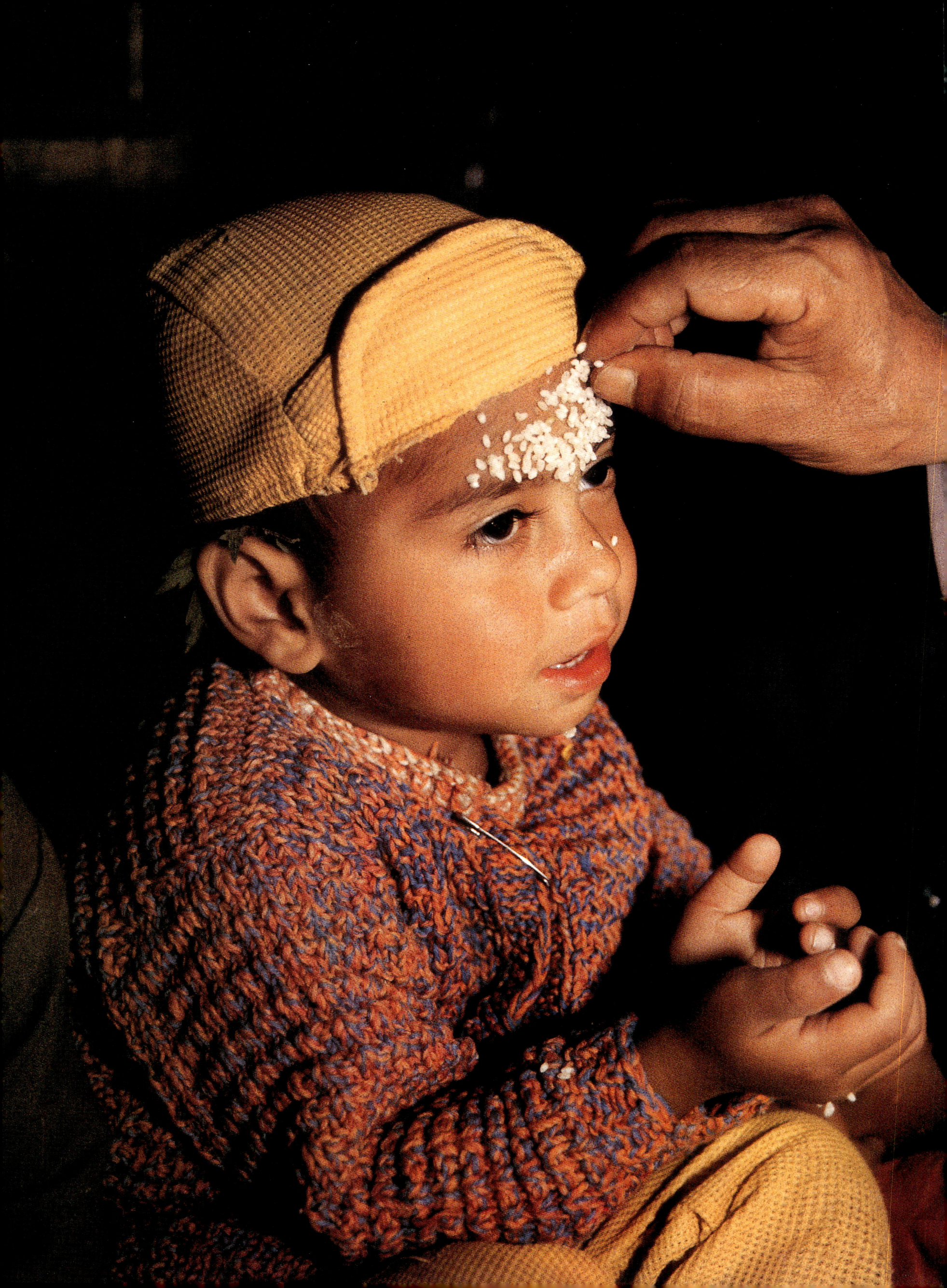

Hinduism

It is only dawn, but clothes are already wet with perspiration. Black clouds whirl in the sky, but no monsoon rains fall yet. No breezes stir the coconut palms and banana trees. Men, women and children walk down the steps into the Sita Kund, Sita's pond, in Nepal's Terai lowlands. One morning thousands of years ago, Sita bathed in this pond that now bears her name; and then married Ram, the incarnation of Vishnu.

Cries of children playing in the cool water mingle with the sounds of clothes being beaten clean on stones. Women modestly wrapped in saris dip into the water while bare-chested men rub themselves clean with handfuls of salt.

In their midst stands a man thigh-deep in the water. He is a Brahmin, distinguished by the sacred thread draped over his right shoulder and across his thin bare chest. His white cotton *dhoti* clings to him. Eyes shut to the red rising sun, he quietly recites in Sanskrit as his hands sweep the air in ritual gestures.

The spiritual and the mundane coexist here. This is what Hinduism says, that the gods walk among us, that they live ultimately in each of us.

Hindu blessings can take many forms and often have counterparts in Buddhist practice. A Hindu father blesses his son with curd and rice in Sikkim (facing page). Rice symbolises the harvest, and yogurt the sacred cow. Newars of Nepal, whether Buddhist or Hindu, share similar customs, such as using milk in initiation rites (left). Nepalese girls receive a 'tika' blessing (top right) on the Buddha's birthday. This red dot also symbolises the third eye of all-seeing wisdom. For Hindu women, it is more of a cosmetic (top left). Water has much significance in Hinduism, cleansing the physical and spiritual impurities of this holy man bathing in the Bagmati River, Nepal (above), and carrying away the ashes of the cremated (far left) and leading their souls to heaven.

Buddha's Middle Way

Neck bells clanging, a line of yaks reaches Tibet's Shung La Pass. Shrill whistles and well-aimed stones drive them forward. Even after a lifetime here, the herders breathe with difficulty in the thin air. At the summit they pull out thin flags — red, green, yellow, blue and white — printed with the Sanskrit mantra '*om mani padme hum*' (hail to the jewel in the lotus). They string the flags into a line and add it to the dozens of lines already there, some faded, some still bright.

The herders move on. They turn back to watch their prayer flags in the ever-present wind. They know the power in those flags and in the words written on them. Each flutter sends the prayer, a salutation of praise to the Avalokiteshvara, soaring to heaven. Each prayer sent to heaven this way earns a little more karma for the man who tied the flag.

Rituals and practices based on the *Tantra*, esoteric exercises supposedly passed down by the Buddha, enable devout Tantric practitioners to channel energy to make the leap to enlightenment. Some Tantric exercises are believed to lead to supernatural powers. The Frenchwoman Alexandra David-Néel mastered *thumo reskiang*, or self-heating. In this way she saved herself and her companion one freezing snowbound night. She also witnessed a monk demonstrating *lung-gom*, or flying: 'He seemed,' she wrote, 'to lift himself from the ground, proceeding by leaps. It looked as though he had been endowed with the elasticity of a ball.'

Sadhus and Hermits

To undertake pilgrimage in the Himalayas is a key part of ordinary life, but some Hindus forsake everything in favour of wandering, meditation and teaching. Seeking personal enlightenment, they become pilgrims for the rest of their lives, carrying with them only their meagre possessions.

Dressed in saffron robes or naked but for ashes smeared all over their body, these Sadhus and hermits perform extreme acts of self-mortification, such as burying their head in the sand for hours. Their backgrounds are varied. They can be children, young men who have abandoned wives or businessmen who, having successfully raised a family and founded a business, walk out the door, never to see their family again. Some Sadhus are charlatans, beggars of the worst sort, but many are true saints walking among us.

Self-enlightenment for Buddhists is more of a quiet affair, for the Buddha achieved enlightenment in solitary meditation. Social contact of any kind would detract from the spiritual quest. Across the valley from Muktinath the cliffs are honeycombed with grottos, both natural and man-made, used by lamas intent on solitary meditation. Bhutan's Guru Rinpoche meditated so intensely that his body left an impression on the rock on which he sat.

Dilli Ram (facing page) wandered the Hindu world for decades before settling down in the forest outside Narayanghat between Nepal's Terai and Middle Hills. The 'ashram', or place of retreat, he built offers shelter to society's outcasts — repentant criminals, widows, abused women, street children — or anyone else seeking refuge. At the other end of the spectrum are sadhus who use the institution to make a living. This sadhu (left) uses his skill at yoga to amaze onlookers by performing incredible body contorting 'asanas', or yoga positions. He makes his living this way in Pashupatinath, in the Kathmandu Valley. There are yet other sadhus whose colourful foreheads and ash-smeared faces (top left and top right) contrast with the simple demeanour of Buddhist hermits, like this one at Swayambhunath Stupa, Kathmandu Valley, Nepal (above).

At the crossroads of East and West, the Himalayas are home to another of the world's great religions: Islam. The northwestern Himalayas, which stretch into Pakistan, are mainly Muslim. A man (below left) prays amidst spectacular mountain scenery in Baltistan, also known as Little Tibet. It is part of the Ladakh frontier district in Pakistan and home to the Baltis, a non-Mongol Muslim people. Ethnically Mongol Muslims are found in Tibet (right and below). They act as butchers, a job rejected by Buddhists on religious grounds. The interior of Bara Mosque in Old Lhasa, Tibet, is decorated with tapestries of Mecca (left), while the mosque in Kathmandu, Nepal (far left), adds a touch of Islamic style to the cityscape.

MARKING THE WAY

Every day a festival is sure to be celebrated somewhere in the Himalayan Kingdom. Nepal commemorates both Hindu and Buddhist auspicious events and therefore has the most number of festivals by Himalayan standards.

Almost every monastery in Bhutan has its annual festival that revolves around Buddhist religious events and usually features days of elaborate dancing. Archery contests are also often an excuse to hold a carnival.

Tibetans also love archery, but horse racing contests are even more popular on their vast flat plateau. Almost all other festivals there relate to Buddhist religious observances. Several monasteries hold festivals on the occasion of the hanging of huge *thangka*, or traditional Buddhist cloth paintings. Pilgrims come from far away to attend. Camps and picnics spring up, and drinking, impromptu dancing and mahjong soon follow.

In Nepal holidays are fixed by the lunar calendar. *Mela*, or festivals, are held on the same phase of the moon in the same month each year. People simply gather at the same place, such as by a river. During the day people arrive, set up tents, booths and shops. All night long they gamble, drink, eat, dance, shop and flirt. At dawn many take a holy bath in the river, then head for home. By the evening the clearing is empty and perfectly ordinary once more.

A colourful horse-drawn chariot, accompanied by guards in smart red uniforms, leads a large procession through the streets of Kathmandu, Nepal (left). In the carriage sits a large cardboard portrait of Tribhuvan, the monarch who led the revolt against the Rana regime in 1951. This is one of the many customs marking the anniversary of King Tribhuvan's birthday. In other parts of the country jeeps, trucks or rickshaws are also used to parade the king's portrait.

Tibetan nomad festivals on Trapchi plain, near Lhasa, Tibet, liven up an otherwise bare landscape with colourful horsemen and mounts (left and centre above). Horsemanship is a much honoured skill across the broad flat expanses of the Tibetan Plateau. These festivals are symbols of a culture that is vibrant and respectful of its traditions. Just as popular as outdoor events are indoor board games and gambling (above). Another celebration is the annual unfurling of large thangka paintings in monasteries. This auspicious time is being commemorated here (facing page, top left) with much pomp and ceremony at Gyantse Monastery's Kumbun Chorten.

Losar — Tibetan New Year

For Buddhists across the Himalayan Kingdom the biggest festival of the year is the New Year. Called Losar in Tibet, this three-day celebration of the start of the lunar year is commemorated by festive delicacies, visiting friends and making temple and monastery offerings. Children get new clothes, women set aside their chores and deck themselves in their finery and men huddle over mahjong tables for hours hoping the New Year will usher in new luck.

Early in the morning many families visit their local monastery or temple to make offerings and receive blessings. Inside, huge plumes of incense fill the air. Outside in the temple courtyards brand new prayer flags are strung up, splashing the blue sky with colour. People and lamas gather there and, at a predetermined moment, toss handfuls of tsampa into the air, then at each other. Nobody objects despite being dressed in their finest clothes. Only smiles abound.

In Sikkim the festival is called Lossoong, and is a two-day worship of the mountain god, Kanchenjunga, who is responsible for bringing rains and blessing the land.

There are variations in the way the festival is celebrated throughout the Himalayas, but the essence of it remains the same from Leh to Lhasa, Kathmandu to Thimphu — a celebration of happiness and prosperity, of lives renewed and hope resurrected.

*T*sampa, the offering for New Year, is Tibet's staple food. Throwing the tsampa high into the air in one joyous burst symbolises the removal of all the bad luck and bad memories of the outgoing year (right). As the tsampa falls, a new year begins on a slate wiped clean. Another tradition welcoming the New Year is to put up new lines of prayer flags (centre left). Adding to the sounds of Losar celebrations of exiled Tibetans in Kathmandu are huge horns (above), here blown from Boudhanath Stupa. In Tibet these horns can be heard for miles across the thin-aired plateau.

Indra Jatra

For eight days each September the great festival of Indra Jatra turns Kathmandu into a raucous celebration of ancient luck. Disguised as a mortal, Indra, the God of Rain, descends into the valley to pick flowers. The valley farmers capture him and brand him a thief. His heavenly mother, Dagini, arrives to rescue her son. The farmers relent and release Indra. A grateful Dagini grants them the boon of heavy fogs to water their crops during the dry autumn and winter months. Indra Jatra thus commemorates the farmers' good fortune.

Indra wanders the streets of Kathmandu, vanquishing the demons in ritual dances. The demon Lakhe, with his hideous red mane, bounds through the streets terrorising those in his way, in particular children. Indra's faithful elephant searches frantically for his master. Swinging this way and that he knocks over onlookers in a slapstick comedy. Images of Bhairab the Destroyer, an incarnation of Vishnu, are unmasked and worshipped. His fearsome visage is anointed with flowers and fruit. Rice beer trickles from the mouth of the huge mask of the White Bhairab and men compete for a taste of this lucky brew. Only one will win the luckiest symbol of all, a single fish swimming in the alcohol.

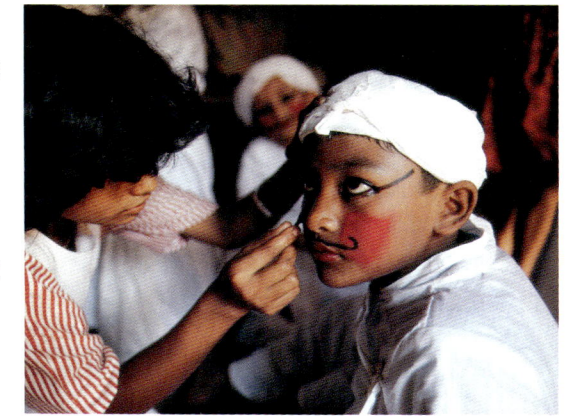

The pretty young girl deemed the living incarnation of the goddess Kumari is pulled through the narrow passes in a wooden chariot with wheels as big as a man. Inevitably power poles are knocked down, roofs demolished and bones broken. The chaos only adds to the raw emotion of this eight-day burst of excitement.

Various characters act out a perennial drama during Indra Jatra: the Kumari dons her finery (centre left); Bhairab, God of Terror, is worshipped in his many forms (right and top left); and festivities in Kathmandu continue late into the night (above). At nearby Bhaktapur, their New Year, Biskhet Jatra, also involves Bhairab. His chariot is dragged through the streets (facing page) amidst much noise and chaos. Boys are the focus at Gai Jatra, when they are first made-up to look like cows (top right) and then paraded through the streets.

FOOD AND LIFE

When people meet on the trails of Nepal the first thing they ask is not 'How are you?', but 'Have you eaten?' Food in Himalayan communities is not only about energy and nutrition. Neither is the pleasure derived from it merely the sensual enjoyment experienced by the gourmet. As with so much of life here, food has a much more fundamental significance, because it is not something taken for granted in this difficult landscape. Trekking across the vast wilderness of the plateau or climbing steep mountain trails, one has to carry one's own food, find a source of water and fuel — the latter usually being dung from the pack animals — before even sitting down to cook.

In village homes, food preparation is a ritual. Water is fetched, firewood collected and dried. Food is cleaned, utensils prepared, spices ground. Like a religious ceremony, preparing food consists of calm, deliberate and repetitive actions. In high-caste Hindu homes, the kitchen is considered sacred. Only those of equal or higher caste are allowed to enter it. In Buddhist homes, all are welcome to sit around the hearth, but a small portion of each cup of tea, of each vessel of food, is tipped onto the fire as an act of thanksgiving to the benevolent deities.

Nomads may spend months on the road, either as traders or herders. Their homes and their kitchens go with them. Weight is at a premium, and few utensils (right) are needed for a trip of two days, two weeks or even two months. Shops may be weeks away, and a man who can cook well with limited ingredients (above) is a much sought after companion. These lamas (facing page) are being served food as part of a purification ceremony in the Nar Valley, one of the remotest parts of Nepal.

Children in Sikkim (above) enjoy special spicy food cooked on the occasion of the Dalai Lama's birthday. Like most Himalayan people, they eat with the fingers of their right hand. Spices are essential in Himalayan cuisine, whether rubbed raw as a flavouring into meat in Kathmandu (bottom left), or boiled with rice in the Khumbu region of Nepal (left) or first dried (below) and then used as a condiment in Paro, Bhutan. Bhutanese cuisine is famous for being spiced with dried chillies.

A Ritual Offering

A Hindu puja sometimes resembles a movable feast. Brahmin priests preside over a vast array of rice, yogurt, milk, coconut, betel nut, bananas, apples, tangerines, several varieties of sweets, cardamom, oil and butter. After the rites are completed the food is redistributed among the worshippers. This is prasad, the blessing from the gods in heaven in return for the lavish offerings. Worshippers will often save a portion of it to give to family and friends who could not attend in person, thereby letting them also share in the blessing.

Altars in Buddhist temples are often crowded with *torma*, elaborate figures and statues sculpted from yak butter and coloured tsampa. Butter is used to light dozens, sometimes hundreds of tiny cup lamps.

At Losar crowds of people dressed in their New Year finery joyously throw handfuls of tsampa into the air and then at each other. A month after Losar comes the Lantern Festival, when huge yak butter sculptures are built along the Barkhor pilgrimage circuit in Lhasa.

Many festivals are marked by specific cuisine. During Dasain, the most important Hindu festival, which celebrates the victory of the Goddess Durga over an evil demon, 12 kinds of meat dishes are prepared from goats sacrificed to Durga. Kwati, a superbly nutritious stew made from six types of beans, is served during Gai Jatra Festival, to decrease the effect of illnesses brought on by the monsoon rains.

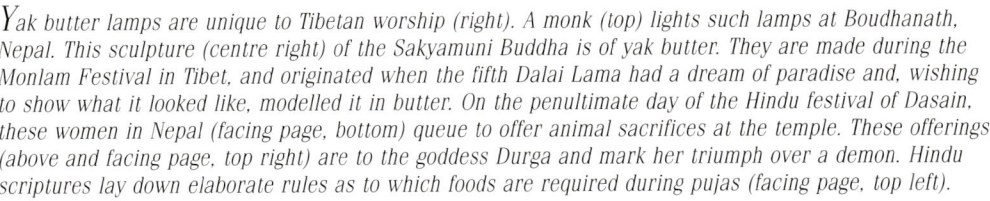

Yak butter lamps are unique to Tibetan worship (right). A monk (top) lights such lamps at Boudhanath, Nepal. This sculpture (centre right) of the Sakyamuni Buddha is of yak butter. They are made during the Monlam Festival in Tibet, and originated when the fifth Dalai Lama had a dream of paradise and, wishing to show what it looked like, modelled it in butter. On the penultimate day of the Hindu festival of Dasain, these women in Nepal (facing page, bottom) queue to offer animal sacrifices at the temple. These offerings (above and facing page, top right) are to the goddess Durga and mark her triumph over a demon. Hindu scriptures lay down elaborate rules as to which foods are required during pujas (facing page, top left).

Rice and Salt Trade

Salt is one of the few resources Tibet has in abundance owing to its past life under the sea. Nepal and India to the south have almost none, but they produce corn, wheat and rice, all in short supply in Tibet. Out of these resources and deficiencies has grown a cross-border, centuries old trading relationship between Nepal and Tibet.

Caravans of yaks take to the high passes, each animal carrying around 50 kilograms of salt, often in bags woven from their own hair. When they reach a major bazaar in Nepal they trade for bags of rice, corn and wheat.

Traders from Nepal journey north to the high villages near the start of the Tibetan plateau, where they can find woven wicker baskets filled with tons of salt, a commodity worth as much as gold to the Nepalese household. Even with the introduction of cheaper iodised salt from India, many Nepalese prefer the flavour of Tibetan rock salt, a few crystals of which are ground on the family spice-grinding stone along with the household's unique mix of curry spices.

Walk the bazaars of Kathmandu and you can see piles of Tibetan salt crystals for sale.

The Drink that Binds

Some of the best tea in the world is grown in the Middle Hills of the Himalayas. Tea is a major part of Himalayan life and drinking tea is how almost everyone starts off the day.

In Hindu and hill tribe culture milk tea is most popular. Milk, sugar, water and powdered tea leaf are all boiled together for a considerable time and then strained into small glasses. The tea can also be flavoured with cardamom, cinnamon and anise. If milk is unavailable, just add extra sugar and lemon or lime juice. If there is no milk and sugar, then ginger, pepper or salt will do just as well. Straight tea is almost unheard of.

The preparation of tea by Tibetans is entirely different. Tea comes in hard bricks of compacted tea leaves. A piece of this brick is broken off and boiled with water. The tea is then strained into a large churn and salt and butter added. The mixture is churned, the churn producing a rhythmic 'whoosh' sound that becomes quite soothing. Tibetans drink tea at any time. Usually a jug of it sits warming by the fire, ready for an unexpected guest, or for the end of chores. It is often taken with meals, something Hindus would never do. Sometimes, mixed with tsampa in a bowl or in the mouth, tea *is* the meal.

Caravans like this (above and top right) of yaks, mules, horses and even sheep, laden with bags of salt and grain are a common sight in a region that is still almost without roads. Rock salt is ground here in a traditional grinder (top left). Many fortunes were once made in the salt trade that linked Nepal and Tibet.

In the Hindu sphere of the Himalayas, milk tea is the norm and is served anywhere from the noisy bazaars of Kathmandu, Nepal (far right), to the manicured lawns (right) of refined public schools in Darjeeling in West Bengal, south of Sikkim.

The 'tea cycle' begins high in the cool tea estates of Sikkim, when women pick choice tea leaves (top left). From here tea travels to the rest of the Himalayas and beyond. In Tibet compacted chunks of tea are sold in Barkhor Market, Lhasa (top right). A woman prepares to churn yak butter tea (centre right) in Bhutan's Mongar Valley, while her Sikkimese counterpart in Bakkhim, Sikkim, is ready to serve hers (above). Bhotia men (left) in Nepal enjoy the final product.

95

A NOBLE OBSESSION

It has all the hoopla and colour of any major sporting event. Team-mates offer shouts of encouragement, the opposing team howls in derision, while cheerleaders lead the spectators in support of their team. The spectators on their part cheer in delight, groan with disappointment, or reward unexpected victory with applause.

Bhutan's national sport is *datse*, or archery, and it has been an obsession for as long as there has been Bhutan. Every village has a *bha cho*, or archery range, where teams shoot at wooden targets placed 140 metres away, compared to the Olympic distance of 50 metres.

There is a tournament somewhere in Bhutan almost every weekend, with two annual national competitions: one using traditional bamboo bows and the other using the latest high-tech equipment.

Competitors at tournaments are all tradition, though, dressed in *gho*, the national dress. An archer who hits his target is rewarded with a unique song and dance by team-mates. A bad shot is rewarded with howls of laughter and bawdy remarks insinuating his lack of sexual competence.

The Bhutanese government encourages young Bhutanese men and women in the sport, urging them to aim for nothing less than an Olympic medal. With centuries of practice and passion backing them up, it would surprise no one to see it eventually happen.

At this archery contest in Thimphu. Bhutan (right), contestants use traditional bows to shoot. At the contest in Paro (top left), the competitors are free to use high-tech, state of the art bows. But whichever type of bow they choose, archers make it a point to wear the traditional Bhutanese 'gho' during the competitions. It is a very practical costume, suitable for both archery and horse riding. The long sleeves can act as gloves, the high hem leaves the legs free and the fold across the front is a convenient spacious pocket.

PART FOUR
ANONYMITY AND DEVOTION

Bhutan's conch-shaped National Museum in Thimphu displays many thangka paintings. They are richly hued in blues, reds, golds, and greens, and fill the walls of several rooms. Some of these masterpieces are hundreds of years old. The museum itself is an architectural treasure and dates to 1656. It is popular with Bhutanese, but they come not only to view the paintings.

Offerings of flowers beneath the thangka paintings scent the rooms. *Torma*, colourful sculptures of flour and butter, are also placed beneath them. Butter lamps add points of gold light. Hands join in prayer. The low murmur of reverent prayers gives an ambience unimaginable in a western museum. In the Himalayas art has always been inseparable from devotion.

Whether it is painting, architecture, sculpture or dance, the purpose of all art is to reveal some aspect of the divine. For example, Tibet's Samye Monastery represents within its circular walls the entire Buddhist Universe, while Gyantse's huge Kumbun Chorten is an enormous three-dimensional mandala. The very creation of art is an act of worship, whether as artist executing the piece or as individual commissioning it. It also adds good karma to our current life, insurance for a better destiny in the next life.

Art is also public. A Himalayan trail follows a roaring river. On one of the huge boulders deposited by the river in a flood long ago is an image of the Buddha. Painted by some unknown traveller, it surveys all who pass by. Whether here or in a temple courtyard, art in the Himalayas invites all to stop, to look, to reflect.

Chiangpur sits along a ridgetop in eastern Nepal. It has a Mediterranean feel with its stone-paved streets, whitewashed homes and courtyards shaded by citrus trees. For centuries its artisans were famous for their brasswork, and even today the sounds of hammer on metal still ring out through the air. In one shop a master sits cross-legged on a mat. He is working in wax on the finer details of an oil lamp to be cast in brass, for use in a Hindu puja. The dish of the lamp features delicately carved serpents. Behind the snake carvings sits a Hindu god, his face serene, his hands in supplication. When this lamp leaves the shop, not a single mark on it will identify its maker.

Similarly, we do not know who fashioned the graceful poses of the statues of Jamuna and Ganga, the river goddesses that flank the doorway of Patan's Teleju Bhawani Temple. In fact, artists are nameless since Hinduism and Buddhism view signing off an artistic creation as indulging the ego, abolishing which is central to both religions. Hence the devotion in anonymity, the beauty in silence.

Art goes public in the Himalayas. In Pemayangtse Monastery, Sikkim (facing page), monks and lay people hang a large thangka kept specially for the annual monastery festival. Large boulders (above) at trail junctions and other key points are often brightly painted with religious themes. Their artists are almost always anonymous.

PROTECTION AND PIETY

The great Buddhist monasteries scattered across the Himalayan Kingdom were designed as both sanctuaries and public houses of worship.

Whitewashed, with monumental inward-sloping outer walls of tightly fitting stone, they shut out the harsh climate and the odd brigand. The buildings drew a clear demarcation between the outside, secular world and the inner, spiritual world of the lamas. Massive and monolithic on the outside, monasteries allowed the monks within to devote themselves to their studies and meditation towards enlightenment. These imposing structures were also a potent symbol of power, both spiritual and political. Today they continue to provide sanctuary in both the physical and mental sense.

The sensation experienced on entering a Tibetan monastery is a powerful one. Leaving behind the stark, wide-open, monochromatic landscape of the Tibetan Plateau, one steps into an explosion of colour. Large wall murals depict fantastic guardians of indescribable fierceness and strength, including Mahakala and Hayagriva, two of eight such Buddhist divinities. These give way to scenes of the Buddha's life and of the serene, pure white Avalokiteshvara. While the vast, bright, openness outside is silent but for the wind, the monastery is filled with incense, drums, cymbals, bells and chanting. It is a truly remarkable experience.

Gompas, or monasteries, are the focal points of Ladakh. They are situated on steep cliffs or high ground (facing page), near water, and away or above ordinary dwellings. Gompas, meaning 'solitary', reflect the Ladakhi worldview of the links between mountain, valley, water and the produce of the land. Monasteries in Bhutan also function as forts and civil centres. Taktsang (far right), Bhutan's oldest monastery, burnt down in 1998 in a fire caused by butter lamps.

Mahakala, the 'Great Black One' (top left), protects the tents of Tibet's nomads and the entrances to monasteries. Away from the throng of pilgrims in the outer public areas, a monastery's hushed courtyards (right) and tranquil rooms provide spaces for study and contemplation (above). A new generation of monks salutes the old (far right) in a monastery at Nepal's Swayambhunath Stupa in the Kathmandu Valley. Tibetans living in exile still retain the gentleness and ready smiles of their nomad counterparts on the vast plateau back home in Tibet.

White Palace, Pure Land

The most memorable structure in the Himalayas is the Potala, the Dalai Lama's palace in Lhasa. Sitting atop 130-metre tall Marpo Ri, or Red Hill, its 1,000 rooms or so rise another 13 storeys until the Potala towers 400 metres above the city. There are over 1,200 years of history here. Long before the Potala, Tibet's first great king Songsten Gampo built his palace here in the 7th century.

There are actually two palaces within the Potala, whose name is a reference to the Avalokiteshvara. The Potrang Karpo, or White Palace, was completed by 1649. The construction of the Potrang Marpi, or Red Palace, within the White Palace, was completed some 50 years later and considerably enlarged the structure.

Though linked, the two palaces were constructed with different functions in mind. The White Palace housed a seminary, a printing shop and living quarters. The newer Red Palace inside the white holds shrines, *stupas* or reliquaries, an assembly hall for monks, and the tombs of eight Dalai Lamas.

The 13th Dalai Lama undertook some alterations in the early 20th century, but the structure has remained basically unchanged since its construction. The Potala was shelled during Tibetan resistance in 1959 and survived the mayhem of the Cultural Revolution when Zhou Enlai reportedly ordered his own troops to guard it. It was unoccupied after the Dalai Lama fled in 1959, until it reopened as a museum in 1980.

The changing moods of the Potala: the palace sits majestically between mountain and lake (facing page), its reflection shimmering in the calm waters; a brooding Potala towers over Lhasa (above), which lies under a blanket of dark grey storm clouds; a close-up view of the White Palace (top left), with the inner Red Palace in the background. One of Asia's most famous monuments, the Potala was once the home of the now exiled 14th Dalai Lama (top right).

Tashi Chho Dzong

Fire and earthquake could not defeat Bhutan's Tashi Chho Dzong, or Fortress of the Glorious Religion. The monastery was first erected in 1216 on a hill overlooking Thimphu by the Tibetan lama, Gyalwa Lhanangpa. He is credited with building dzongs across Bhutan. Later Bhutan's greatest lama, Ngawang Namgyal, expanded the dzong system and turned them into administrative centres as well. At Tashi Chho he built an additional lower dzong to house the civil authorities, while the original apartments continued to house monks.

In 1771 the original dzong caught fire and was abandoned. The rebuilt structure burned a further three times between 1866 and 1962, and suffered an earthquake in 1897 which damaged the central tower. In 1962 King Jigme Dorji Wangchuk enlarged and completely renovated it to make it the seat of his government. True to tradition, no written plans were used, and the wooden portions were joined without nails.

The elaborately painted and decorated walls are superb, with trimmed and fitted granite blocks on the outer walls and beautifully proportioned step-roofed wooden towers at the four corners. Tashi Chho is an excellent example of monumental architecture in the Bhutanese style, and a fitting seat for Bhutan's royal government.

Founder of the Nyingmapa sect to which the Bhutanese royal family belongs, Guru Rinpoche (above) figures prominently at Tashi Chho Dzong (right and facing page, top), now the site of the throne room, king's offices and the national secretariat.

The annual Tsechu dances are in honour of Guru Rinpoche and depict events in his life or reflect on his teachings. Four days of dancing transform Tashi Chho Dzong's tranquil main courtyard (top) into a whirl of costumed saints and demons, clowns and deities. They are watched by hundreds and hundreds of mesmerized spectators (above, centre right and facing page, bottom). Drums (above centre and facing page, bottom), central to the dances' musical accompaniment, reverberate in the stone-paved courtyard. Held on different dates at each of Bhutan's dzongs, the Tsechus at Tashi Chho held in September, are among Bhutan's most spectacular.

Swayambhunath

Long ago the great holy man, Vipaswi Buddha, planted a lotus seed in a beautiful lake. A wondrous lotus bloomed and from it emanated the astonishing blue light of Swayambhu, the primordial Buddha, represented by a pair of all-seeing eyes. Far to the north the hero Manjushri saw the light and came to worship. He cut the hills bordering the lake with his flaming sword of wisdom. The lake drained, leaving behind the Kathmandu Valley, while the lotus settled on its roots and formed the hill of Swayambhunath, one of the two most sacred Buddhist sites in the valley.

Looking east across the valley is the other sacred site, Boudhanath. The story of its origin is equally poetic. A young goose herder asks the king to grant her all the land a single buffalo skin can cover. He laughingly agrees, whereupon the girl cuts the skin into thin strips, ties them together, and strings the rope around the area eventually occupied by the present-day stupa.

In recent years it has become the centre of the Tibetan community that fled to Nepal after the Chinese takeover. It is a leading centre for Tibetan studies, with monasteries of the Sakyapa, Nyingmapa, Kagyupa and Gelukpa sects all within the vicinity of the stupa.

A monkey (right) swings in front of Swayambhunath's all-seeing eyes, which overlook the Kathmandu Valley. Between the eyes (facing page) is the Nepali symbol for the number one, 'ek', which symbolises the unity of all things. The steep climb from the base of stupa (below) up 300 stairs does not discourage devotees from coming to worship at its sacred dome (top left). The Boudhanath Stupa (left) across the Valley was bathed one evening in the warm glow of thousands of yak butter lamps, lit for the cremation rites of a prominent lama.

NEWAR ARCHITECTURE

During the rule of the Malla dynasty in Nepal, from the 10th to the 18th century, the three city states that shared the Kathmandu Valley — Kathmandu, Bhaktapur and Patan — underwent a cultural renaissance that produced what is arguably the most stunning architectural heritage in the Himalayas. This architectural style characterises many sacred and secular Nepalese buildings, and is named after the Newar craftsmen of the valley who were its main proponents.

Central to Newar temples are multi-tiered roofs of diminishing size, which create the illusion of exaggerated size and height. This illusion is aided further by placing the temple on a series of diminishing plinths. The temples are built in brick, a plentiful resource in the valley. Windows and doors have exquisitely carved wooden frames and screens. Roofs are usually made from clay tile. Their heavy projecting tiers are supported by another unique feature: elaborately carved wooden supports that run from the sides of the walls to the eaves. The most ornate temples have a *gajur*, or pinnacle, of gilded copper.

Two- and three-tiered roofs are the most common, but two examples of five-tiered roofs exist: Patan's massive Khumbeshwar Temple, enlarged to five tiers in the 17th century, and Bhaktapur's Nyatapola Temple.

The classical Newar design crossed the Himalayas when the 13th century Newar architect Arniko took his group of 24 assistants to Beijing, to serve in the court of the Ming emperor. Many think that the pagoda style ubiquitous to East Asia originated in Arniko's work.

A brilliant example of Newar style is the five-tiered Nyatapola Temple (facing page), towering over Bhaktapur, Nepal. This shrine to goddess Siddhilakshmi is the one of the tallest in Nepal and built so solidly that only the top tier was loosened in the great 1934 earthquake. Each pair of carved figures on the steps represents ten times the strength of the pair below. Newar style, with its elaborate window sills and frames (above) and roof supports (right), is composed on the back of intricately carved details such as these 'vajra', or thunderbolt, patterns (top left).

The Eastern Masterpiece

Changu Narayan sits on a ridge overlooking the city of Bhaktapur in Nepal. It is the crowning jewel of dozens of architectural gems scattered throughout the Kathmandu Valley.

Narayan is Vishnu's incarnation as creator of the universe. Each cardinal point on the circle of mountains surrounding the valley is marked by a shrine dedicated to him, with the greatest, at Changu, marking the east. The present shrine dates to about 1700, but there has been a temple here since at least the 4th century.

Changu Narayan is a classic two-tiered Newar temple with beautifully carved wooden roof supports. The entrance is covered in intricate repoussé metalwork, while the temple courtyard is full of sculptural masterpieces. There are several representations of Vishnu: as the lion Narsingha disembowelling a demon; as the dwarf Vikrantha, transformed into a giant and crossing the universe in three strides; and as Narayan reclining on the multi-headed naga king, Ananta.

The Garuda statue near the entrance has a human face which many take to be that of Manadeva, the founder of the 5th century Licchavi dynasty in Nepal. Nearby is a pillar dated to about the middle of the 5th century. The inscriptions describe Manadeva's military achievements and is Nepal's oldest extant historical record.

This 5th or 6th century sculpture at Changu Narayan outside Bhaktapur, Nepal, shows two incarnations of Vishnu (far right): the erect figure is ten-armed, ten-headed Vishnu slicing through the universe of a thousand demons with his ten weapons, while the reclining figure below is Vishnu resting from his strenuous labours on a bed formed by the coils of serpent king, Ananta. As brilliant as Changu Narayan's individual details are (right), much of its beauty comes from the way the stone, metal and wooden elements all come together to create a stunning vision of art (above and top left).

Patan's Durbar Square

A European visitor at Patan's *durbar*, or palace, square in the 1920s described it as 'the most picturesque collection of buildings that has ever been set up is so small a space by the piety and pride of Oriental man'. Housing more than 30 monuments in a comparatively small space, with a further 30 close by, Patan's Durbar Square is acknowledged as the best preserved and most vivid example of classical Newar architecture in an urban setting.

Entering the complex from the south via the Sundari Chowk courtyard one sees within it what is possibly the most beautiful royal bath in the world. The walls of the sunken bath are covered with row upon row of magnificent carvings of Hindu deities. The sunken bath is shaped like a *yoni*, the symbol of female sexuality, and abounds in 'eights'. Its eight sides proclaim the king's devotion to the eight naga rain goddesses. Statues lining the tank represent the eight Bhairab incarnations of Shiva and the eight Ashta Matrika mother goddesses who attend to Shiva. Shiva himself with his consort Parvati rides Garuda on the brass water spout.

Outside, at the northern end of the square, is Bhimsen Mandir. This large and squat temple is dedicated to Bhimsen, hero of the *Mahabharata* and famous for his Herculean strength. Three-tiered, richly furnished and well-kept, it also highlights Bhimsen's other role of patron of business and commerce.

Close by is the 17th century Krishna Mandir, unique in being one of the few temples to feature an Indian *shikhara*, a bullet-shaped dome. Built entirely of black stone, it stands in contrast to its brick-and-tile neighbours, and its solid mass overflows with a boisterous river of pilgrims come the night of Krishna's birthday in autumn.

Patan's old name was Lalitpur, meaning City of the Arts. Her medieval Malla kings, determined to outdo their relatives ruling Kathmandu and Bhaktapur, set out to create a beautiful palace looking out onto a square filled with equally beautiful temples. Their success is still visible today (above). The square boasts a rich contrast between Newar style brick temples and the Indian-inspired stone ones that feature shikhara towers (top left). Amidst the monumental architecture are smaller works such as stone elephant sculptures (right) and 'torana' — gorgeous wooden carvings above doors and windows (top right).

SCULPTURE

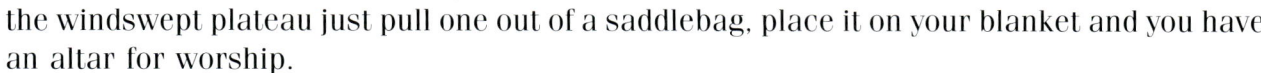

Metal, wood, stone, butter, clay — artists worked with all these materials to produce masterpieces. All across the Himalayas they worked in anonymity, according to the dictates of their religion. The art they produced was mainly religious. Even secular figures are depicted in acts of worship, as seen in the monumental pedestal-mounted sculptures of Malla kings in Patan and Bhaktapur.

Given the nomadic nature of Tibetan life, most of their masterpieces are little objects, which are small enough to be easily packed and carried, for example *ama dablams*. These ornate cases are superb examples of decorative metalwork and are designed to hold an image of the Buddha. Far out on the windswept plateau just pull one out of a saddlebag, place it on your blanket and you have an altar for worship.

In forest-rich Nepal and Bhutan wood is a favourite medium. Metal is another choice and Nepal's artists have always been masters of repoussé — the art of stamping, chiselling, and hammering designs into the reverse side of a sheet of metal such that the designs appear in relief on the front.

The barren Tibetan Plateau gives few opportunities to work in wood, so Buddhist sculptors there work in butter. For larger creations they use a wooden frame around which the butter is sculpted. Sometimes the butter is mixed with tsampa and coloured. The impermanence of the sculpture, an echo of life, is part of the art. Hindu artists working in Nepal's Terai lowlands have a similar tradition, producing wonderful clay images of gods and goddesses for festivals. Following the end of the festivities the image is carried to a river or pond and sunk.

A stone lion stands guard by a statue of a Hindu deity in the heart of medieval Bhaktapur, Nepal (above). Monumental sculpture is common in the towns and cities of the Kathmandu Valley because of the abundance of stone in the valley. Religious figures are also the subjects of visual representations in Tibet, where butter sculptures pay homage to the lives of saints (top right) and finely-turned metal sculptures of the Sakyamuni Buddha (top left) and Padmasambhava (centre left) decorate monastery altars.

Vessels of the Eternal

Sculptures both large and small are usually portrayals of deities. One of the greatest monumental statues in the Himalayas is the Sleeping Vishnu at Budhanilkantha in the Kathmandu Valley. This massive, five-metre long, black stone image of Vishnu is depicted as sleeping in the coils of the serpent Sesha. It was probably carved outside the valley and then, incredibly, pulled in and submerged in the spring in which it now rests.

Most Tibetan and Bhutanese sculptures are small-scale objects used for religious rituals. To stress the impermanence of life Tibetan sculptors often incorporate human bones into their work. The top of a human skull may be turned into a ceremonial drum, or a bowl lined with silver and rimmed with an intricate silver motif.

Small figures of bodhisattvas or protector deities are often carved hollow. A piece of scripture is then placed inside the hollow. This adds to the statue's powers. Whether made in Bhutan, Nepal or Tibet, these small figures are crafted down to the minutest detail. The best pieces have gold gilt.

There is also a tradition of monumental sculpture in Bhutan and Tibet. Large figures of the protector deities often guard the entrance to altars. Examples at Lhasa's Jokhang Temple are the Hayagriva and Vajrapani sculptures that flank the entrance to the shrine of Amitabha, the Buddha of Infinite Light.

Statues, once completed, contain the essence of the divine, quite literally in Tibet, where the hollow interiors of statues are filled with rolls of scripture (centre right). Public art is the object of public worship (centre left and far right): Milk is offered to the Sleeping Vishnu of Budhanilkantha, Nepal (top), while butter lamps adorn the serene face of Maitreya Buddha in Ladakh's Thiksey Gompa (right).

In Relief

A temple or monastery often seems like a cross between a house of worship and an art museum. Most of the best sculptures are still used as objects of worship, while some others double as structural supports and decorative feature.

The wooden struts used to support the heavy roof overhangs are a favourite canvas for Newar artists in Nepal. Adorned at times with fierce animals, at others with beautiful figures or erotic lovers, they encompass a myriad subjects. At the beautiful Man Kamana Temple in central Nepal the struts even cover the rare theme of daily life.

Perhaps the most beautiful Nepalese Buddhist monastery is Uku Bahal in Patan. Built in the 17th century, the decorative metal arch framing the main door is a masterpiece, while the courtyard leading to it displays a wonderful menagerie of carved animals both real and imagined. Nearby is Kwa Bahal whose facade is covered in repoussé figures. One of the finest examples of Newar repoussé work is the Sun Dokha, or Golden Gate, built in 1753 for Bhaktapur's royal palace. Made from sheets of gilded copper, it has been favourably compared to Ghiberti's famous doors of the baptistry of Florence cathedral.

A Gurkha soldier stands guard at Bhaktapur's Golden Gate (top left), considered by many to be the most beautifully crafted gateway east of Florence. Ornate embellishment is also a common theme in Tibetan and Bhutanese decoration and flat surfaces like roof eaves and wooden pillars are covered with colourful lotuses, chrysanthemums, poppies, swirling clouds, mythical beasts and geometric patterns (right, above, and centre left). Newar decoration of Nepal can sometimes feature erotic art (top right).

Chortens and Mani Walls

The Tibetan name for stupa is *chorten*. Chortens were built to hold the cremated remains of the Buddha, so old is their history. They are still used as a repository for religious relics, holy scriptures or the remains of lamas and holy men. Chortens may look simple, but they have a highly developed iconography. The base is a three-dimensional mandala and represents the earth. The dome signifies water, while the spire rising above, fire. Near the top of the spire the sun and moon represent air and space. At the very top a seed symbolises enlightenment.

Mani, or jewel, walls line the trails of even the highest Himalayan mountains. Every stone in these walls boldly displays the mantra 'om mani padme hum'. Each mani stone is carved or commissioned by an individual to gain karma for the next life. When a stone is carved, the mantra goes skyward to the Buddha, who is referred to in the prayer as the jewel in the lotus. By placing the stone in the open breeze the prayer continues forever. Rarely taller than a man, mani walls are collections of mani stones, and become longer as each pilgrim adds his or her own stone offering. These stones and walls are reminders of the path to enlightenment. Like a chorten, they should always be passed to one's right.

Chortens and stupas are common features across the landscape of the Himalayas and Tibet. To suddenly come upon a chorten in a remote spot — whether in the lush jungles of Pemayangtse, western Sikkim (far right), or by barley fields surrounded by desert mountains in the Zanskar Valley, Ladakh (above) — is to be reminded that we are surrounded by the divine as we struggle on our journey towards enlightenment. Mani stones and mani walls along paths (top left) are also visible signs to the pilgrim that he or she is on the right road, that the protection of the gods is still forthcoming and that the goal is not far. Extra karma is gained for this carver of mani stones (right) beneath the Potala in Lhasa, for she allows the buyers of her stones to gain merit when the stones are eventually laid out along pilgrim paths.

ORIGINALITY WITHIN CONVENTION

In Bhutan's School of Arts and Crafts dozens of small boys sit on the floor modelling identical images of the Buddha. In another room dozens more copy a mandala, striving to replicate a well-worn original.

They are expected to master a complex iconography, not develop an original style. The centre of the Wheel of Life must contain the snake, pig and cock. The left foot of the Green Tara must rest on a lotus. The hero Manjushri wields in his right hand the flaming sword of awareness. His left hand holds the scriptures in a lotus blossom, adopting the teaching *mudra*, or gesture, one of the six main hand gestures in Buddhist iconography. All these conventions have meaning.

The young boys work busily, memorising the age-old techniques and compositions. They come from all over Bhutan and are sponsored by the government. Upon graduation they will return to their village homes to keep alive Bhutan's artistic traditions.

In Tibetan art too artistic conventions must be followed. If painting the *bhumisparsha* mudra, which signifies victory over the demons' temptations, the Buddha always sits on a lotus throne. He is identified by 32 specific marks on his body. His hair is blue, his right hand hangs down touching the lotus throne, while his left rests palm up on his lap. Any deviation would be anathema.

The arts are not an easy path to follow. Originality comes from working within the restrictions of iconographic conventions, with the artist ever wary of expressing in his work the ego so detrimental to spiritual enlightenment.

Buddhist monks and lay people unfurl a giant thangka of Guru Rinpoche during Tsechu festivities at Wangdi Phodrang Dzong in Bhutan (centre right). Once the thangka is unfurled against the monastery's high walls, monks gather to chant in front of it, while butter lamps are lit beneath it and lay people surge forward to touch the sacred painting (below). While large thangkas are eminently suited for mass devotion, small thangkas are preferred for private meditation (above).

Thangka Paintings

Thangka paintings are traditional cloth paintings of Buddhist images. They can vary from the size of this book to pieces large enough to drape across the facade of a three-storey building. The smaller sizes are mounted on a brocade background and rolled up around wooden handles, like a scroll. The word *thangka* in Tibetan actually means 'something rolled up'. Thangkas are convenient to carry in Tibet, the land of nomads. The larger thangka paintings are usually unfurled only once a year at temple festivals, such as the annual festival at Shigatse's Tashilhunpo Monastery. Thangkas may depict the Buddha, saints or the Wheel of Life, but the mandala is perhaps a more common subject.

Mandalas

Mandalas represent the cosmos, whose chaos is overcome by its geometric design. In the centre of the mandala is a focal element that represents the centre of the cosmos. A common central figure is Avalokiteshvara. Through meditation, the two-dimensional mandala emerges as a three-dimensional cosmos, with the central figure ordering the chaos around it.

The word *mandala* derives from the Sanskrit word for 'circle'. Mandalas developed as aids to meditation, representing not only order and harmony, but also the multiple layers of mystery found in our human existence. Many see in them universal images that reflect basic human instincts. This has given them an attraction that has spread far beyond the Tibetan Plateau.

A Bhutanese mandala (top left) at Rinchepung Dzong depicts the Cycle of Cosmic Creation. Another mandala (left) shows Shambala, the heavenly city of those of good faith. Mandalas are the work of skilled experts (top right), who are often descended from generations of painters.

Mural Paintings

The decorative painting of Tibetan monastery walls is a specialised school of art. Murals are a dense abstraction of ever-changing geometric and floral patterns, swirling clouds, lotus flowers, swastikas and auspicious symbols, all in a phantasmagoria of colour. Elaborate portraits of bodhisattvas, guardian deities, Guru Rinpoche and Milarepa fill the walls with their threatening or forgiving faces.

Here, as in thangka painting, there exists a strict and complex iconography. Usually there is a central figure surrounded by other figures or scenes from the central figure's life. It is in these surrounding figures that the artist is allowed the most latitude of style and content. In the mural depicting Milarepa's life in Bhutan's Paro Dzong, for example, the surrounding scenes are so large and elaborate that they share the mural in equal proportion with the central portrait.

The paintings are often a team effort. Once the apprentices have completed the basic figure, the master fills in the details, especially the hands and face.

The serious student of Tibetan mural painting has many splendid examples which he can copy and study (centre right): the wall painting (left) inside Lo Gekhar Monastery in Mustang, Nepal, depicts Hayagriva, a protective deity, who through sex with his consort finds release of Tantric energy; entrances to monasteries frequently depict protecting deities such as these Guardians of the Four Directions (above) at the entrance of the National Museum in Paro, Bhutan; the perpetually turning Wheel of Life is a favourite theme in Buddhist art and these examples are from Tongsa Dzong, Bhutan (facing page), and Lhasa, Tibet (top left).

The Wheel of Life

Travelling throughout the Himalayan Kingdom, you are bound to see the Wheel of Life if not on a thangka, then at least at entrances to Buddhist monasteries. The wheel is a visual reminder of how our desire traps us in the endless cycle of birth, death and rebirth.

Hideous in his crown of skulls, Yama, the Lord of Death, grasps the wheel with his leering mouth. The outermost circle of the wheel depicts the 12 experiences common to life. In the intermediate wheels are six sections representing the six realms of rebirth. The three upper realms of rebirth house the gods, titans, and humans; the three lower ones are for hungry ghosts, hell, and animals respectively. In the innermost circle are three animals: the cock, the snake and the pig. They symbolise desire, anger and ignorance and are painted chasing each other's tails in an endless cycle.

Yama, Lord of Death, clutches the Wheel of Life (above and facing page). The outermost 12 sections depict our 12 experiences in life. In the innermost circle a cock (desire) devours a pig (ignorance), who in turn devours a snake (anger). The 6 sections in the middle depict the 6 realms of rebirth in which we are seemingly trapped. But in each realm the Buddha preaches a way to escape the clutches of Yama, and thereby flee the Wheel and gain enlightenment.

Tibetan Sand Paintings

Tibet's artists work in all the traditional materials: stone, wood, metal and cloth. But they also work in butter, flour and sand. Sand paintings reflect the Buddhist belief in the impermanence of all life. When they are completed they are typically allowed to remain a few days, and then simply brushed away into nonexistence.

Composed out of any number of colours blended with sand, they are a complex, minutely detailed work executed by a group of monks over a number of days. They are usually laid out in conjunction with a religious observance.

A group of lamas visiting the USA worked several days on a sand painting. Just as it neared completion, it was damaged. The monks simply smiled, shrugged and started again. No, the loss of several days' work did not bother them, they said. It was, in fact, the point and a good lesson learned.

Monks in Bhutan (above and centre) completed this sand mandala in two weeks. The laying out of a sand mandala requires concentration, as a slight quiver of the hand, even a mis-aimed breath, could ruin the whole painting. The art is a good indication of the discipline and concentration needed for the practice of meditation. A slip of the hand is also a chance to show emotional discipline, and to laugh in the face of stress and anger. Painting on rocks (left) is also a form of religious and artistic expression, this example from Sera Monastery, Tibet.

*Y*oung monks (facing page, centre) accompany the dances on drums. They use long sticks with a curving striker at the tip. When struck with these sticks, the drums create a steady pulse that fills Bumpthang Monastery's courtyard in Bhutan and keeps the whirling Black Hat dancers in time (right). The dancers form a mandala with their steps. The long skirts and sleeves exaggerate the proportions of the swirling dancers (below) and create a meditative, almost hypnotic mood for the spectators. Individual characters, like Yamantaka the Destroyer, also keep audiences spellbound, as at Swayambhunath's Nyaling Pengaling Monastery in Nepal, where a lama (facing page, bottom) reprises the role of Yamantaka in scenes from the judgment of the dead.

WHIRLS OF COLOUR AND PASSION

A horde of demons in bright robes swirls through the air. They pause only to sneer through hideous fangs. A lone hero sword in hand, tosses back his long black hair, then strikes. Drums reverberate, cymbals clash and the demons cringe and cower before the all-consuming wrath of the righteous hero. Goodness prevails and evil is vanquished.

Like every other art form, dance in the Himalayan Kingdom is attuned to the divine. It portrays morality at its most basic: Good fights Evil, Good vanquishes Evil, and finally gives birth to enlightenment.

The dances reach into history and mythology celebrating the stories of gods and heroes, of strong men who follow the right path and find enlightenment, and of weak men who lose it and along with that, their souls.

Part entertainment, part sermon, dance is the perfect medium to reach out to all, from children, farmers and nomads to monks and lamas. People watch, eyes wide open, as supernatural figures in magnificent costumes and monumental masks move with restrained grace or frantic passion.

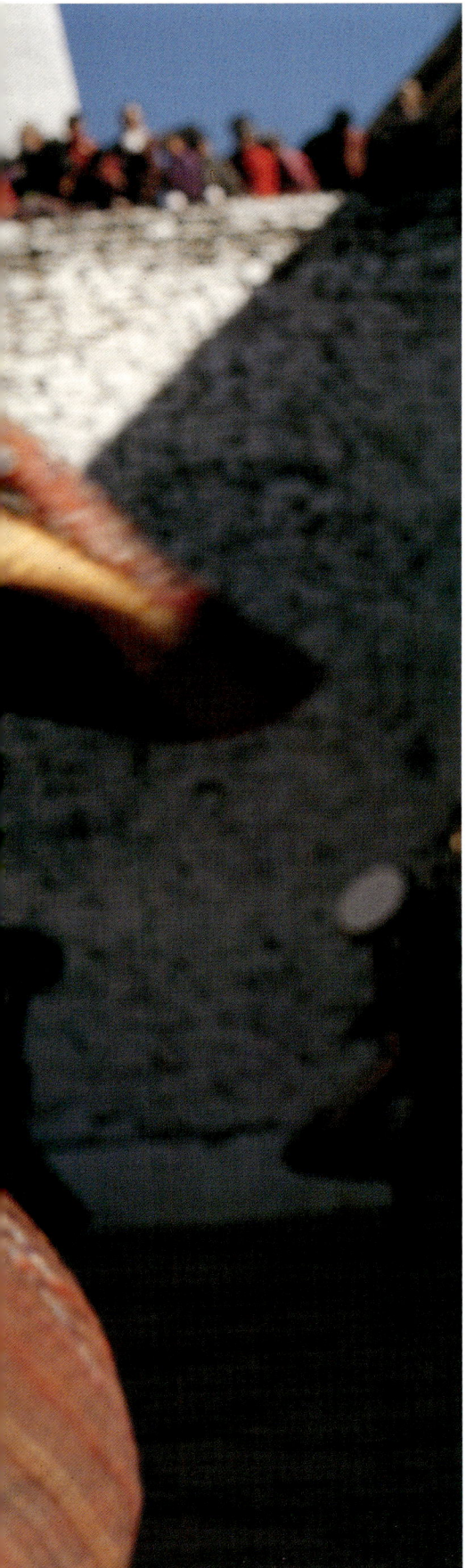

Tibetan Cham Dance

Cham, or a dance performance, is a feature of many festivals in Tibet. At its most basic cham depicts the exorcism of malign spirits. The authority presiding over this performance is a Black Hat lama who is the only dancer to remain unmasked.

The Black Hat is surrounded by lamas wearing masks that transform them into manifestations of various guardian deities. A human effigy, made from dough, wax or even paper, represents the evil force the lamas are assembled to combat.

Cham is a spectacular drama that takes place over several days. Massive long trumpets, drums and cymbals accompany the solemn movements of the dancers around the effigy. Each motion and gesture of the dancers has significance. At the climax of the dance the effigy is destroyed and evil symbolically vanquished.

Cham has been interpreted as having several levels of meaning. Some view it as a representation of the ancient struggle between an anti-Buddhist king of the Yarlung Valley and the monk who eventually slew him. Some see the dance as dramatising the establishment of Buddhism in Tibet. Others see it as a metaphor for the struggle within each of us against evil.

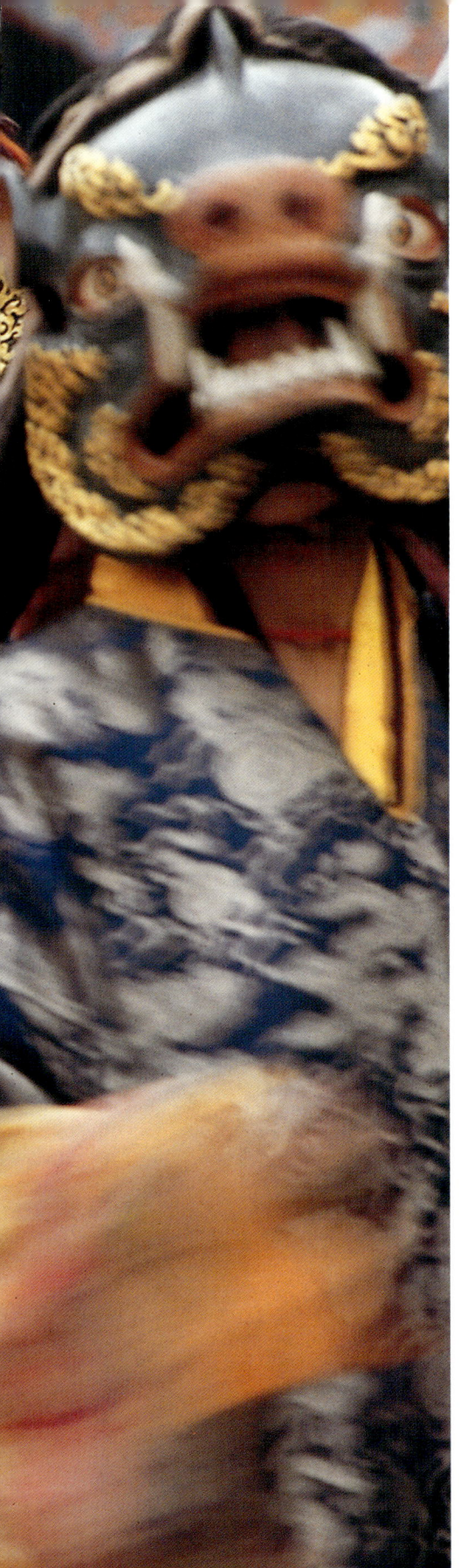

Tsechu

Most dzongs in Bhutan put on performances of *Tsechu*, a series of dances that recounts major events in the lives of the great figures of Drukpa Kagyu Buddhism. These dances usually concern the great Guru Rinpoche, the founder of the Nyingmapa sect and a major figure in Tibetan Buddhism. His two journeys to Bhutan had a profound effect on the growth of Buddhism there. The *Gere Tshen Gyed* dance dramatises the eight manifestations of Guru Rinpoche.

Other dances follow the life of Milarepa, the great hero and poet beloved throughout the Buddhist Himalayas. The *Shawo Shachi* dance depicts how the simple hunter, Gonpo Dorji, transforms into Milarepa himself.

Many of the dances were personally composed by Shabdrung Ngawang Namgyal, the great 17th century leader of Bhutan. Others were envisioned by Pema Lingpa, a great lama who lived slightly before the Shabdrung and who was one of the five great *terton*, or discoverers of Buddhist treasures. Through their dances, these venerated figures bestow a blessing on all spectators. At the same time the dances demonstrate that the dharma protects and rewards its followers

All is not solemn and righteous preaching, though. *Atsaras*, clowns, are a major part of the dances. They stop the scene from becoming too serious. With their comic routines and masks with prominent noses, they are a real crowd pleaser.

Tibet is not the only Himalayan region known for its dancing. Dance is also an important part of life in the south. Small villages in remote Nar-Phu, Nepal (below centre) hold a cycle of cham dances during religious feasts. Jankris are Nepalese faith healers (bottom left) and use dance to drive away sickness and disease. Young women in traditional dress dance to welcome an important visitor to Lachung in Sikkim (bottom right).

Sherpa's Mani Rimdu

The most famous hill people of Nepal are the Sherpas. Living in the area south of Mount Everest, they have become synonymous with skilful high altitude portering and climbing.

The Sherpa Festival of Mani Rimdu symbolises the fight between Bon and Buddhism. Before Buddhism became entrenched in Tibet, it had to contend with Bon, the more ancient animistic religion that is still practised in pockets of the Himalayas. In fact, many of its features have been assumed into Buddhism, most obviously prayer flags and spirit traps. The struggle against Bon was hard but Buddhism eventually triumphed, and Mani Rimdu dramatises this victory in three days of dancing.

The festival is held twice a year. On the full moon of May or June the dances are staged in the monastery at Thami. Normally a quiet corner of the Sherpa world, Thami overflows with people arriving for this performance. Six months later the dances are staged again at Tengpoche, the most famous Sherpa monastery, which also happens to be situated directly on the trail to Mount Everest.

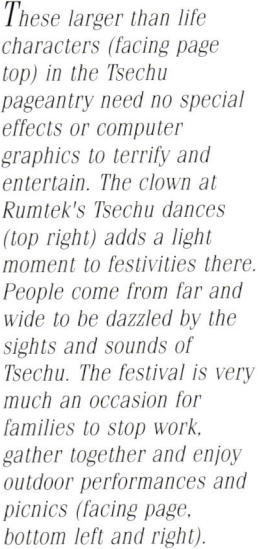

These larger than life characters (facing page top) in the Tsechu pageantry need no special effects or computer graphics to terrify and entertain. The clown at Rumtek's Tsechu dances (top right) adds a light moment to festivities there. People come from far and wide to be dazzled by the sights and sounds of Tsechu. The festival is very much an occasion for families to stop work, gather together and enjoy outdoor performances and picnics (facing page, bottom left and right).

A LIVING TRADITION

Walk the streets of Patan's Hauga neighbourhood in the Kathmandu Valley and your ears will soon be ringing with the sounds of hammer clanging on metal. Peek into a doorway and you will see men sitting cross-legged on the floor. They work with hammer and chisel pressing intricate designs into the sheet of metal they hold and manoeuvre with their feet. Not five minutes away, in a much quieter workshop that opens into the narrow courtyard of the 16th century Maha Baudha Temple, a master puts the finishing touches on a wax figure. He holds his piece up to the light for a final check.

In the villages of eastern Bhutan you will often hear the sound of a loom hammering warp and weft tight as women weave designs of dazzling intricacy. Most weaving is done the traditional way, with a backstrap loom. One end of the loom is attached around the weaver's back by a strap. With the other end of the loom fixed, the weaver leans back against the strap to keep the warp tight.

All across the Himalayan Kingdom you can find women weaving in wool or cotton, sometimes even silk, making everything from luxurious Bhutanese *kushutara* dresses to ordinary woollen *bhuku* wraps. The Gurung hill tribe depends on the latter to keep dry during the monsoon and warm in winter. In Tibet woollen carpets and saddle blankets are still a household necessity for the country's nomads. These are still produced in the home, as well as in more modern carpet factories.

Whether woollen carpets or brass statues, wooden carvings or elaborate embroidery, the tradition of handicraft continues to thrive in the Himalayan Kingdom.

Bhaktapur's famous potters still sell mainly to the local Nepalese market. Their centuries old potting techniques have hardly changed. This woman (bottom centre) dips each pot into the vat of glaze in front of her. A young potter in Bhaktapur (below) learns the skill his family has practised for hundreds of years. Child labour is common in the Himalayan Kingdom, with many children working beside their parents and siblings.

Once upon a time, Nepalese wood carvers worked (above and top left) on the windows and doors of wealthy traders and royalty, but these days tourists are their main market (facing page, top right). Tibetans once wove only for their family, making carpets for their beds, sofas and houses. Today Tibetan-style carpets are Nepal's leading export and largely done by non-Tibetans there. Carpet manufacture in Lhasa, Tibet, is carried out in large mechanised factories employing modern equipment (facing page, top left). In Bhutan, a smiling girl (facing page, bottom) still relies on the traditional wooden loom to create her pieces. Like the Nepalese boy potter (far right), she too makes a valuable contribution to her family's monthly income.

HIMALAYAN KINGDOM
SACRED ART OF THE MIDDLE WAY

This image of the Sakyamuni Buddha, or Sakya Thupka, gazes down at pilgrims inside the Jokhang in Lhasa, one of Tibet's holiest Buddhist shrines. He is surrounded by bodhisattvas, his left hand holds a begging bowl while his right hand touches the ground in the 'bhumiparsha' — calling the earth to witness — gesture.

Mahakala, the 'Great Black One', is a Tantric deity and has links to the Hindu god Shiva in his incarnation as Bhairab the Destroyer. Mahakala is considered the fierce manifestation of Avalokiteshvara, the Compassionate One, and was the personal deity of Kublai Khan. Here he is depicted amidst the flames of hell, brandishing the limbs and heads of those who are caught in his power through their practice of vice.

This Bhutanese painting portrays the great Guru Rinpoche, also known as Padmasambhava. Founder of the Nyingmapa, or 'red hat' sect, he was famous for his use of Tantric magic and rituals to defeat demons that threatened him. He sits here with a tiger on his lap and is protected from the evil demons around him by the small talismanic parasol he holds in his right hand.

*P*aintings of the Sakyamuni Buddha must depict both his humanity and his divinity. Seated on the lotus throne, he holds a myrobalan plant in his right hand. It is a medicinal plant symbolic of Sakyamuni's healing powers. His left hand holds a begging bowl filled with three blossoms. A halo surrounds his blue hair. The protrusion from his topknot, his elongated earlobes and the dot on his forehead are also signs that he is the Enlightened One.

This mural from the Dalai Lama's former rooms in the Potala show scenes from the monastic life. Great lamas teach and advise their disciples. Tantric knowledge in particular is handed down orally from master to student. Theological debate was, and still is, a regular form of mental exercise among Buddhist monks. In the painting the beautiful gardens within the monastic compound are filled with flowers, ponds and birds and provide the perfect atmosphere in which to cultivate the soul and mind.

The lotus flower, here shown decorating part of the roof of a Buddhist monastery in Nepal, represents the Buddha's purity and compassion. These perfect attributes rise above the muddy waters of our earthly existence, above our imperfect words and deeds. On the lotus sits a book of sacred scripture and above that is the sword of awareness. This flaming sword cuts through the ignorance than engulfs the world.

The 'lokpala', or protectors of the law are significant figures in the Tibetan pantheon. Among the most important are the four guardian-kings of the cardinal points. On the left in the Lord of the West. Red-faced, he holds a chorten in his left hand and a snake in his right. On the right is Vaishravana, Lord of the North, who holds a mongoose in one hand, and raises in the other a banner celebrating the victory of the Buddha's teachings over evil.

The great Milarepa, who wandered the Himalayas in the 11th century, is famous as a magician, saint and poet. He is one of Tibet's greatest heroes and remembered for his joyful singing and teaching. His poems and adventures are very well-known even today. Milarepa's body is usually painted green because he is known to have eaten nothing but green nettles. His name translates as 'cotton-clad', after his simple garments. In paintings he usually holds his hand to his ear, indicating the accurate pitch of his singing.

The Tara, or saviour, was born from a tear shed in compassion by Avalokiteshvara, the Bodhisattva of All-Encompassing Compassion. The White Tara above is associated with the day. She sits in the full lotus position displaying her most visible attributes — her seven eyes (palms, soles of feet and forehead) — which together represent the insight she embodies. Historically she is said to be Wencheng, the Chinese wife of Tibetan king, Songsten Gampo (A.D. 618-49), who helped convert him to Buddhism.

Sakyamuni meditated for six years, renouncing physical needs and almost wasting away. He mastered fear, controlled his body and mind, but enlightenment still eluded him. He realised that enlightenment could not come from austerity alone and, accepting this bowl of curds from the maid Sugata, he began his search for 'the middle way' that eventually led him to become the Buddha, the Enlightened One.

The Four Friends, one of Bhutan's favourite stories depicted on the walls of Sera Monastery in Lhasa, Tibet. The elephant, monkey, peacock and rabbit can do nothing on their own, but cooperating together they can succeed: the peacock plants the seed, the rabbit waters it, the monkey fertilises it and the elephant guards it. When it produces fruit they stand on each other's backs and heads and pick enough fruit for a veritable feast.

A mural at Thiksey Gompa, outside Leh in Ladakh, depicts a famous local Tibetan lama whose holiness and wisdom attracted even some of Ladakh's Muslims. They are represented in the bottom right of the picture by the bearded figure with a turban who respectfully raises his hands to the lama. The lama is sitting in semi-lotus position and has a halo of enlightenment. New wealth from tourist visits allows this great monastery to preserve and restore many of its artistic treasures.

*T*his beautiful mural from Lakhang Monastery in Ngatshang, Bhutan, is striking for the way it allows the viewer to appreciate the details of the larger than life motifs. A seemingly simple composition belies the arguments conveyed by the subtly exaggerated proportions. The huge chain, the snarling mouth and bulging eyes of the tiger, the strained stance of the keeper indicating both his strength and that of the tiger, the stylised and overblown clouds and flowers — all these could contribute to a story of how a strong virtuous man is able to master his inner passions.

This mural at Gantey Gompa in Bhutan is awash with gorgeous colours and fine details. Above the blue Mahakala sits a serene, enlightened being. The contrast between the two supernatural figures is played out in colours and symbols: the demon is surrounded by the orange-vermillion flames of hell, while the enlightened being sits on a verdant throne which sprouts lush foliage and pink, blue and red flowers; the demon has skulls and symbols of death around him, while the enlightened one is surrounded by life-affirming symbols.

A smorgasbord of characters adorn this wall also in Gantey Gompa, Bhutan. The composition of the painting is typical of Himalayan Buddhist art. A central figure is surrounded by various other paintings which are either different incarnations of the central figure, or scenes of events or people connected to his life. The detail that goes into the narrative is extraordinarily complex. To the expert each minute detail, each colour, each gesture of the characters, speaks volumes. To the lay person the overall vision is one of stunning virtuosity and poetry.

The great Shabdrung Ngawang Namgyal (1595-1651) is the subject of this mural at Bhutan's Tashi Chho Dzong. He is one of the most important figures in Bhutan's long history. He is renowned as a teacher, politician, administrator and painter. He laid the foundations of today's Bhutan. Here he is surrounded by saints and deities. Such is his wisdom that even the animals of the forest, as represented by the deer, are enchanted. The screen on the lower half of the mural protects it from the reverent touch of lay people.